All to One Another

All to One Another

The University at Home and in the World

ANDREW A. SORENSEN

PUBLISHED FOR THE OFFICE OF
THE PRESIDENT OF THE UNIVERSITY OF SOUTH CAROLINA
BY THE UNIVERSITY OF SOUTH CAROLINA PRESS

Published by the University of South Carolina Press for the
Office of the President of the University of South Carolina
Columbia, South Carolina 29208

www.sc.edu/uscpress

Manufactured in the United States of America

17 16 15 14 13 12 11 10 09 08 10 9 8 7 6 5 4 3 2 1

Library of Congress Cataloging-in-Publication Data

Sorensen, Andrew A.
    All to one another : the university at home and in the world /
  Andrew A. Sorensen.
        p. cm.
    ISBN 978-1-57003-773-3 (cloth : alk. paper)
    1. Sorensen, Andrew A. 2. University of South Carolina—
    Presidents. 3. Education, Higher—Aims and objectives. I. Title.
    LD5022.S66 2008
    378.757'71—dc22   2008013735

This book was printed on Glatfelter Natures, a recycled paper with
30 percent postconsumer waste content.

For Arturo Aaron Sorensen, who brings me great joy

Contents

Contents

Personal Coda

Preface

AS WE NEAR THE END OF THE FIRST DECADE of the twenty-first century, our institutions of higher education are challenged to harness the energy, intellect, and enthusiasm of our faculty and students. They are increasingly desirous of international mobility in their academic pursuits, and their enthusiasm is paralleled by the substantial growth in partnerships among universities in the farthest flung corners of the globe. The role of university presidents in this rapidly changing milieu is to nurture supportive synergy among this increasingly diverse and dynamic base of constituents—defining the strength of common goals and not losing focus while applying that strength to the betterment of the whole. These are, without question, lofty goals during what are indisputably trying times for the academy. Issues of accountability, accessibility, and rising costs in the face of reductions in federal and state appropriations for our universities place great demands on higher education's most effective leaders. The changes wrought by the unending technical revolution and growing ethnic diversity, coupled with xenophobia fueled by the threat as well as reality of terrorist attacks—to say nothing of students with learning styles as varied as their cultural heritage and cocurricular interests—come together to create a climate of ceaseless challenge on our campuses.

In the center of the academy's response to that "new order" is the university president donning a wardrobe of hats, from officially licensed ball caps to elegant chapeaux to mortarboards. The university president's role is remarkably varied to say the least. He or she must be a preacher, a teacher, a cheerleader, a scholar, a diplomat, a warrior, a peacemaker, a coach, and a shepherd— depending on the relevant objective or the purpose of the occasion. The university president is the one who asks why, the one who often says yes and frequently no, the one who seeks and finds common ground with a firm commitment to the goals of the academy while making a difference that will last after his tenure is over.

This book is a collection of some of my messages during my tenure as the twenty-seventh president of the University of South Carolina. These words and themes reflect the array of events, tasks, and audiences we university presidents encounter. While the topics vary, their common theme is hope for the future through expanding our vision of the university.

Faculty members teach thousands of students during their lives' work, but they transform minds one at a time. This collection of speeches and articles sketches the multifaceted work of a college president striving to enable faculty and students to reach their full potential. My hope is that each individual entry leads the reader to a more informed understanding of "All to One Another: The University at Home and in the World."

Acknowledgments

I AM ESPECIALLY GRATEFUL to the many people who have reviewed the articles and speeches collected in this book. My most understanding critic is my wife, Donna. She has been unstinting in her support of me as I have wended my way through the labyrinthine corridors of university administration, and I am indescribably devoted to her. Her support and wisdom have been absolutely invaluable, and words cannot express adequately my debt to her.

Several colleagues, as well as the many audiences to whom I have addressed these remarks—all too numerous to mention—have made significant contributions to the writings collected here. Any inadequacies in spite of their suggestions are mine alone.

Finally I have been blessed with two devoted colleagues who made this publication possible: Celia Hartman and Joyce Murphy, my assistants at the University of South Carolina. Their shepherding of this manuscript from start to finish has been essential to its completion.

PART ONE

The University

Remarks at a Memorial Service for Six Carolina Students and a Clemson University Student Who Perished Together in an October 28, 2007, House Fire

OUR UNIVERSITY TOUCHES the lives of many people—just as countless friends shape the role of our university throughout the world. To some this campus is a place of reflection that offers respite from the hectic rhythm of our daily lives. To others it is an invigorating force instilling in all who come near it renewing energy, knowledge, and ideas. But in either case this university is not an island separating its citizens from the rest of the world. Rather it is a powerful force connecting us all to one another.

Carolina is a community of strength. We Gamecocks share a common creed—the Carolinian Creed—dedicated to personal and academic excellence. Our mutual respect for its many core values pulls us together

—to become one family although we are composed of thousands of individuals from wonderfully diverse backgrounds. Among the many individuals in the entire Carolina community, I speak today most directly to the parents and families involved in our profound tragedy.

In all, seven vital young lives have been given up, six from Carolina and one from Clemson. They departed this life in that horrific burst of natural force—a force as unforeseen and unforeseeable as one can imagine. In its wake it became our responsibility to grieve, to remember, to heal, and to move forward without forgetting what might have been.

We honor them not only for the wealth of talent they embodied but perhaps more importantly for the gifts they so selflessly shared with the world around them. We deeply respect what they might have accomplished in their bright futures. Jim Barker, president; Gail DiSabatino, vice president for student affairs; George Smith and Joy Smith, associate vice presidents for student affairs —all from Clemson University—join with us here to mourn their passing.

We also recognize and respect those Carolinians who so narrowly escaped this tragic accident. We give our special consolation to their extended families, SAE brothers, and Tri Delta sisters, and honor their brothers and sisters throughout the student body—and in the respective communities in which they grew up—who share the burden of our grief with unique intimacy.

We salute Justin, Travis, Lauren, Cassidy, Will, Allison. We shall never forget the vitality they brought to our campus, to our Gamecock family, or the positive influence they had on the lives of countless friends. We shall carry with us their joyful pursuit of new experiences, unprecedented growth, and new beginnings.

Now it is we who must continue to pursue new beginnings. We live in a world shaped in part by these spirited young people. We must live up to the expectations they had for their fellow students, their faculty, and all who are part of the University of South Carolina.

We must move forward remembering what they would have asked from us, remembering why they came to this cherished haven of knowledge and progress and action. They are now forever part of our heritage and thus part of the momentum that compels us to continue our mission.

The scripture these six Carolina students and Clemson student held close proclaims clearly: "For everything these is a season, a time for every matter under heaven: a time to be born, and a time to die; a time to plant, and a time to pluck up what is planted; a time to kill and a time to heal; a time to break down and a time to build up; a time to weep and a time to laugh; a time to mourn and a time to dance. . . . "

This memorial service is our special time to join hands as two university communities rich in tradition and remembrance, as well as hope and foresight and action. This is our time to cherish what is past and our time to accept the challenges bestowed upon us by those who are no longer in our midst.

Carolina and Clemson will continue to be improving and great universities. Although we are unquestionably diminished by these losses, let us affirm boldly that our lives will be enriched through having been touched by those whom we remember today. We give thanks for the time they spent among us, and we pray for the perseverance and courage to fulfill their highest hopes for us.

I leave you with a special blessing, which seems particularly appropriate here and now: "Life is short, and we do not have much time to gladden the hearts of those with whom we move along the way. So be swift to love; make haste to be kind; and may the peace of God be with you, and with all whom you love, indeed all your brothers and sisters near and far, both now and always."

AMEN

NOTE

I am indebted to Tommy Stepp for several phrases in these remarks.

TWO

◞

The State of the University Address

THE NUMEROUS CRANES AND BULLDOZERS at work in the Innovista, to say nothing of the emerging biomass generating station on Sumter Street, the Horizon Center research facility on Blossom Street, the Discovery Center Biomedical Sciences Laboratories on Greene Street, and the new Honors College building at the corner of Main and Blossom—these structures give inescapable evidence that we have a building boom going on all around us. Alumni who come back to visit and parents of our students—including the more than one thousand who attended receptions at our home and on the Horseshoe over Parents Weekend—invariably comment on how dramatically our campus is growing. But our growth in facilities must be paralleled by growth in the quality of education we offer.

Our threefold plan for attracting and retaining our state's young people is simple: first attract the most talented high school students to our university; second give them a first-rate education so that they can acquire the skills to perform intellectually challenging yet financially rewarding jobs; and third stimulate the growth of companies within the state that require a sophisticated work force so that our graduates will have ample employment opportunities.

Let's look at each phase of this threefold plan. The data from our incoming students demonstrate unequivocally that the first phase is working. The quality of the 3,690 students enrolled in the freshman class at Columbia this fall is the best in the history of the university—their 3.9 high school grade point average and their SAT average of 1185, up fourteen points from last year, are the highest in Carolina's history.

This is made more remarkable by the fact that last year across the nation there was a seven point decline in average SAT scores, and our state had a six point decline. Our entering freshman class average high school GPA has risen for six years in a row, bucking the national trend. While we increased the size of the fall freshman class only slightly (by sixty-three students), the number of applicants went up by more than one thousand—to a total of more than fifteen thousand—causing the ratio of applicants to openings to be 4.1:1, the highest in our history.

Similarly impressive gains in the quality of incoming students have been reported by USC Aiken, USC Beaufort, and USC Upstate. Thanks to the Education Lottery scholarships, far more of South Carolina's best high school seniors are opting to stay in the state to attend college, and USC is attracting more than its fair share of them. Of the South Carolina students who enrolled as freshmen at Columbia this fall, 98.5 percent received financial assistance from the lottery. In fact 80 percent of our undergraduates in Columbia are from in state, and on each of our other campuses the percentage of in-state residents is even higher.

The University of South Carolina at Columbia has truly become a "destination of choice." Over the past four years, we have kept the size of the incoming class of the Honors College relatively constant while maintaining their average SAT score around 1400. I congratulate Dean Davis Baird and his colleagues for their excellent work.

The Capstone Scholars, an innovative living-learning program in only its second year, enrolled an impressive 488 students in 2005, its first year, and this fall it grew by 28 percent to 625, with an average SAT score of 1299. I congratulate Dr. John Spurrier, who is doing marvelous work as the Capstone principal.

It's essential that our university—on all our campuses —continues to dedicate itself to educating all South Carolinians and not just those who come from families that can afford the extracurricular activities and tutorial programs clearly associated with higher grades and test scores. Thus I'm pleased to report that nearly one-quarter of our Columbia students receive Pell Grants, which are linked to low family income. The *Journal of Blacks in Higher Education* recently reported that in a state where the average family income of African Americans is substantially lower than that of white families, the University of South Carolina at Columbia—with a 15 percent

African American undergraduate enrollment—ranks number one among all fifty public flagship institutions throughout the United States in the proportion of black students.

Our ability to increase the academic quality of our students while concomitantly enhancing access to our university system for all South Carolinians truly sets us apart. It is a success story for the rest of the nation. Although it is abundantly evident that we are attracting outstanding students, I am particularly pleased that our new admissions process looks beyond standardized test scores and grade point averages.

Three years ago I asked our admissions committee to develop a holistic process that was more sensitive to students whose extenuating circumstances merit more careful consideration than just looking at those numbers. Consider the case of one of our students starting at Columbia last year, who had no siblings living at home and whose single mother had to undergo multiple surgeries each year during his high school career. He often had to stay home from school to care for her, and keeping up with his academic work was a real struggle. Some semesters he did poorly. During his senior year, he participated in a health careers program sponsored by his high school. As he excelled in the program, he became passionate about nursing. When his mom told him to apply to USC, he was shocked. He told her he might not get in. Even if he did make it, he argued, they wouldn't be able to afford college anyway. His mother insisted: "Go ahead and apply." He did and was admitted as a nursing major.

The university Financial Aid Office then worked with him to construct a financial aid package to attend Carolina. Now he has a chance to pursue his dreams and embark on a career to help others. We have countless other stories like his, which time does not permit me to relate.

We are also attracting highly talented students to our graduate professional programs. This fall the South Carolina College of Pharmacy, the result of a melding of our College of Pharmacy with the pharmacy program at the Medical University of South Carolina, welcomed its second class of 190 students from a pool of 666 applicants, giving a ratio of 3.5 applicants for each opening. All admitted students were given the choice to enroll here or at the Charleston campus. The majority of them—three out of every five—chose to be on the Columbia campus.

Our Law School reported the highest average LSAT score for the entering class in that school's history and had 1,995 applicants for 215 openings—9.3 applicants for each slot. Dean Jack Pratt is off to a terrific start as head of this school. Our School of Medicine also has become increasingly competitive. Dean Don DiPette reports that this entering class had the highest test scores and grade point average of any class since the school's inception in 1975 and had 1,940 applications for 85 openings, a ratio of 22.8 applicants for each slot.

And last month the *Wall Street Journal* ranked our Moore School of Business number nine in the world for its international business excellence. This month *Business Week* ranked the Moore School number three among all U.S. business schools for the "fastest return" on our

M.B.A. students' investment. For the past ten years our undergraduate international business program has been ranked number one by *U.S. News and World Report.* Year after year *U.S. News and World Report* ranks our international masters in business administration as number one among all public universities in the nation.

The second phase of our plan is to give our students a first-rate education. It is imperative to remember that teaching and learning are at the heart of our mission. But we are increasingly sensitive to the fact that academic success is not limited to classroom and laboratory settings or the library. Each group of students who enters these hallowed halls is more sophisticated about technology than its predecessors. For good or for bad, our students have been bombarded from the cradle onward with an array of visual and auditory stimuli that most of us in our own collegiate years never even dreamed of. Through the ubiquity of the Internet, iPODs, DVDs, Treos, video games, instant messaging, cell phones, and a veritably endless succession of technological inventions, they come to us with expectations that are shaped by those phenomena.

To help our students take advantage of these developments but at the same time enhance their ability to progress academically, we have opened the Student Success Center, housed in the Thomas Cooper Library. This center includes a number of programs aimed at helping all students, but especially those in their first year, to apply themselves and succeed.

I came to this university with the announced goal of enabling any undergraduate who is so inclined to engage in original research. Dr. Harris Pastides responded to this proposal by developing the Magellan Scholars Program, for which we recently named our second cohort. Our university now has a total of 173 Magellan Scholars with one-half million dollars annually to support their research and scholarly projects. These projects span all academic disciplines and are being carried out under the supervision of faculty mentors who have generously given of their time. We'll announce the third round of Magellan Scholars next spring, another expansion of our commitment to research opportunities for our undergraduates.

Our launching of the Magellan Scholars, the Capstone Scholars, the Center for Teaching Excellence, and the Student Success Center—as well as our nationally recognized University 101 program—combine to improve the undergraduate learning environment. Its high quality is reflected in our students' success in winning national scholarships and fellowships.

This past academic year we had nine Rotary International Scholars, four Fulbright Scholars, two Goldwater Scholars, one Truman Scholar, seven Gilman Scholars, two National Security Education Program Scholars, two Tau Beta Phi Scholars, two National Oceanographic and Aeronautics Administration Hollings Scholars, two Freeman-Asia Scholars, one National Science Foundation Research Fellow, one U.S. Department of Homeland Security Scholar, and one EPA Scholar. What an impressive array!

The success rate of our students competing against the best and brightest in our nation's elite institutions is remarkably impressive, greatly facilitated by the thorough preparation they receive from our faculty and staff, who have played a critical role in their outstanding performance.

But providing a first-rate education requires that all aspects of the campus environment be oriented to healthy, productive students. Under the leadership of Dr. Dennis Pruitt and his team, we have developed a comprehensive approach to wellness, whose theme is "Healthy Carolina on My Mind." This program ensures that we address the spiritual, physical, psychological, and financial needs of our students. Among the elements in the overall goal of our Healthy Campus 2010 are initiatives in campus safety and disability services, alcohol and drug abuse and gambling, and tobacco use. All these activities are elements of our "Guide to Wellness." USC Upstate recently launched a comparable campuswide initiative.

While it is critically important for us to provide a rich learning environment for our students, it is also essential that we address the pedagogical needs of our faculty. All our faculty are superbly qualified in their respective academic fields, but many could benefit from understanding more about how new technologies may enhance not only their teaching but also the remarkably expanding learning environment outside the classroom and laboratory. Through Provost Mark Becker we have created the Center for Teaching Excellence in the Thomas Cooper Library, in order to improve our collective response to these expectations. Professor Jed Lyons, of our Department of Mechanical Engineering, is serving as its director. We have also established the Arts Institute, designed to pro-mote collaboration among faculty and students in the arts and humanities and to make their programs increasingly accessible to students and faculty in other fields.

In responding to strong enrollment across the USC system, this year we hired 214 new faculty in Columbia, 60 new faculty in the senior institutions at Aiken, Beau-fort, and Upstate, and another 18 new faculty in our regional campuses at Lancaster, Salkehatchie, Sumter, and Union. The quality of those we are recruiting in all these positions is truly remarkable and bodes well for con-tinued improvement of learning opportunities for our young people.

In addition to replacing more than two hundred fac-ulty who are retiring over the next few years, through the Faculty Excellence Initiative and the Centenary Plan, we are continuing to add significant numbers of new faculty. Those recruited through the Faculty Excellence Initiative are often hired in theme-specific clusters transcending several disciplines. Moreover we are on target to add to our ranks one hundred research faculty who are being recruited through the Centenary Plan. These recruit-ments are focused on research in next energy, nanotech-nology, biomedical sciences, and environmental sciences.

The extraordinary success of this program is illustrated in the quality of faculty we are securing. Among those who joined our full-time ranks this year are people we recruited from the following institutions: five from lead-ing private institutions (Columbia, Chicago, Harvard, and two from Johns Hopkins) and six from prestigious public universities (the Universities of North Carolina, Minnesota, Illinois, Texas–Austin, and two from Michigan).

In spite of the effectiveness of this impressive array of academic offerings, we have a critical statewide mission beyond the borders of our respective campuses. Many people in South Carolina are looking to our state's research universities to be engines of economic development —to help bring about the transformation to a knowledge-based economy. The third phase of our plan responds to this expressed desire by attracting industries spawned by the knowledge revolution so that we may increase substantially the number of high-paying, intellectually challenging jobs in this region.

As a former high school teacher and Presbyterian pastor, I fervently hope that many of our students will enter the human services sector, which is not distinguished by highly compensated jobs. But many of our students have acquired the skills to perform intellectually challenging yet financially rewarding jobs and want to work in the fields for which they are prepared immediately after graduation. I am pleased to report that the plan to create high-tech positions for them is working.

The first step in this process is to have our scientists and engineers who are making inventions to disclose them to our attorneys. The number of these disclosures each year has nearly doubled over the past four years, going from forty-eight to eighty-four, with most of the growth occurring in the past two years. Our attorneys then file a provisional patent application, which offers protection of the invention for a maximum of one year.

At the end of that year, we either apply for a full patent or drop the application. The number of provisional patent applications per year has increased fourteenfold over the past six years (from six to eighty-four), while the number of full patent applications over the same period, which predictably lag behind provisional applications, has trebled (from fourteen to forty-two per year), indicating a dramatic upswing in the entrepreneurial activity of our faculty.

This marked change in our faculty culture is corroborated by the quadrupling of licenses and options signed each year over the past five years (from five to twenty) and by the noteworthy upsurge in license revenues—a nearly sevenfold increase from $59,000 in 2002 to $406,000 in 2006.

Quite predictably all these initiatives are resulting in faculty startups of new companies, going from zero in 2002 to five in 2006. In these ventures we have often taken an equity position in lieu of license revenues. Creating enterprises that build on the scientific discoveries of our faculty is critically important to our state's economy because we can't expect our most talented students to stay in South Carolina if there aren't enough positions requiring a sophisticated labor force to keep them here. Our hope is that all our research initiatives, including the Innovista, will help to create jobs that will make it attractive for these young people to be employed here after their graduation.

Now a word about our support from the General Assembly. I am enormously pleased to report that this last legislative session—my sixth as president-elect and then president—was by far the best for USC. My primary goal for the next legislative session is to continue securing pay raises for our richly deserving faculty and staff. In addition to providing most of the funds needed for an average 3 percent pay raise, we received an additional $4 million in recurring funds for hiring additional faculty on the Columbia campus and noteworthy increases in the budgets of each of the other seven institutions.

We need to continue expanding our IT infrastructure as our uses of electronic technology expand exponentially. Thus we were pleased to receive $3 million for our OneCarolina initiative and another $1.5 million for the Light Rail initiative, which will enable us to link to the National LambdaRail—a countrywide IT network. And for the fourth consecutive year, we secured an additional $30 million for the Endowed Chairs Program, to be shared with Clemson and MUSC.

All of these supplementary funds, coupled with substantial and unparalleled increases in the budgets of all seven of the other USC institutions, are of paramount importance. The number of additional recurring dollars from the General Assembly is without precedent in my tenure here.

I offer special thanks to the heads of the other USC institutions, as well as the leaders of the student government associations at all eight of Carolina's institutions, for their unstinting and highly effective efforts to secure local legislative support for our budget requests. Under the coordination of the Columbia SGA president, Tommy Preston, and Marsha Cole, executive director of the

Carolina Alumni Association—with the able leadership of past president Rita McKinney and current president Bill Bethea, and our board of trustees, we have mobilized our faculty, staff, students, and alumni to make a compelling case for our university's needs. The results of their coordinated lobbying is transparent.

While we have ample reason to celebrate the accomplishments of the past several years, we must not rest on our laurels if we wish to sustain this momentum. Among the most notable challenges before us are these:

+ We must persuade our legislature to make greater investments in our state's young people. They are the leaders of tomorrow.
+ As the Lehman Brothers team who visited us recently pointed out, we must maintain the delicate balance between increasing tuition revenues while making our education accessible to all South Carolinians.
+ We must continue to search for innovative ways to meet the scholarly aspirations of our students and faculty.
+ We must maintain parallel emphasis between creating new facilities for our faculty, staff, and students—from state-of-the-art research labs to smart classrooms to accommodating residence halls—while not neglecting the massive deferred maintenance problems we have.

This is obviously only a partial list, but if we approach these problems thoughtfully and in concert, I am fully

confident that we shall successfully meet these challenges.

This is truly an extraordinary time in our university's
history, and I thank each and every one of you for making
it so.

THREE

Remarks to the University's Women's Studies Twentieth Annual Conference

ON BEHALF OF THE FACULTY, STAFF, AND STUDENTS of the University of South Carolina, I extend a warm and hearty welcome to the Women's Studies Program Twentieth Annual Conference. It took a long time for the white males who dominated the American professoriat from its inception to wake up to the fact that women and people of color are absolutely essential to higher education, and that the future of our institutions rests on the shoulders of women and men of all races, creeds, sexual orientations, and other characteristics by which we typically distinguish ourselves from one another.

I began my professorial career at a historically black university and then sequentially taught at two women's liberal arts colleges—parenthetically, an increasingly endangered species. One of the women's colleges had a male president, and in both of these schools more than half the faculty were men. I am delighted that we have seen substantial changes in the gender composition of faculty not only in women's colleges but throughout the academy in the forty years since I received my first university appointment. But we continue to do an inadequate job of establishing opportunities for women and people of color in all administrative ranks of our universities and colleges as well as in the professoriat. And contrary to the opinion of the most recent president of a prominent institution in Massachusetts, I most emphatically and categorically reject his allegation that women are genetically inferior to men!

I am a huge believer in leadership by example, and that begins at the top. I became president of the University of South Carolina in the summer of 2002. Since then the number of tenured or tenure-track women faculty members has risen by more than 21 percent! During precisely the same period the number of men who are tenured or tenure track dropped by 9 percent. In other words the proportion of women has gone up by more than one-fifth and of men has gone down by about one-tenth. We're not where we need to be, but we're making progress. We obviously don't have final numbers for next fall because recruitment is currently under way for the upcoming academic year, but I fully expect that those trends will continue year after year.

Another way of leading by example is offering opportunities in our administrative ranks. When I became president of this university four and one-half years ago, there were only four women as senior administrators: Jane Jameson, vice president for human resources; Mary

Ann Parsons, dean of the College of Nursing; Pat Moody, dean of the College of Hotel, Restaurant, and Tourism Management; and Shirley Mills, director of Government Relations. After Mary Ann Parsons retired, I named Peggy Hewlett as her successor. During the past four years, we merged the College of Liberal Arts with the College of Science and Math, and I appointed Mary Ann Fitzpatrick as dean of by far our largest faculty, the College of Arts and Sciences. I also appointed Donna Richter, dean of our Arnold School of Public Health; Shirley Carter Staples, director of the School of Journalism; Samantha Hastings, director of the School of Library and Information Sciences; Madilyn Fletcher, director of the School of the Environment; Christine Curtis, vice provost; Elise Ahyi, assistant provost; Rosemary Booze, associate vice president for research; Michele Dodenhoff, associate vice president for university advancement; and Deborah Beck, director of the university Student Health Center. Thus in a period of four years we went from four to fourteen women in senior administrative positions. Each of these persons is the first woman in the history of this university to hold her position.

As a result of the above decanal appointments, more than 55 percent of our tenured and tenure-track faculty and the overwhelming majority of department chairs and institute directors report to women. As these deans acquire administrative experience, it is my hope that—in spite of what is often an extremely hot seat, dealing with conflicting claims from competing constituencies and long days that stretch into long evenings—they will choose to become university provosts and presidents. The message to all our faculty, staff, students, and alumni reflected in the appointments of these ten additional senior women administrators during the past three years is very clear evidence that we value highly the leadership women provide.

I wish you well in all your endeavors, and trust that we will all work together to establish greater prominence for the field of women's studies and provide leadership opportunities for women in every nook and cranny of higher education.

PART TWO

The University in the Community

FOUR

◌

Remarks to the Greater Columbia (South Carolina) Community Relations Council

AS SOON AS I BECAME PRESIDENT of the University of South Carolina three years ago, I asked several African American faculty and staff about the relationship USC had with the black community. I was told that it had been up and down, and that things could be much better. After meeting individually with several African American community leaders to discuss these issues, I appointed a community advisory committee consisting of representatives of the NAACP, the Urban League, local government, our black alumni association, and African American pastors and opinion leaders. At the same time, I reached out to the larger African American community, especially through churches and other organizations.

I was told early on that the Community Relations Council (CRC) was one of the most important organizations in Columbia because its members are working to bring about positive change in the areas of fair and better housing, meaningful employment, and mentoring programs for our at-risk youth. I want to congratulate the CRC on your forty-one years of service to our community. Because of your hard work, your compassion, and your commitment to creating a just society in order to bring about social change, Columbia is known as a place of opportunity, of harmony, of peaceful change, a city where leaders work side by side to discuss differences and seek solutions to problems . . . where everyday folk reach out to one another. The CRC motto is: "Race relations is everybody's business." Because all our businesses should be equal opportunity employers, support for the work of the CRC must come from every sector of the community, including government, business, other outreach agencies, faith communities, and grassroots activists.

It is ironic that this past month we have been bombarded in the media with stories about justice denied in the relentless pursuit of justice for all. Civil rights cases that remained unsolved for more than forty years are finally coming to trial once again, and justice—at long last—is being carried out as we approach the fortieth anniversary of the Voting Rights Act. Forty years ago the struggle was about justice, freedom, and basic civil rights. The struggle was in the streets, and this city was in the midst of that struggle. Mayor Lester Bates and Mayor Pro Tempore Hyman Rubin were determined that Columbia was not going to become a hotbed of violence and hatred. They helped found the Columbia Luncheon Club, which held its first meeting on our university campus in November 1963 and continues to meet on our campus to this day.

While we have not completely won the battle for justice, for freedom, and for civil rights, we have made huge gains during these past forty years. As we celebrate these successes, we need to remind ourselves that, although the struggle is no longer in the streets, the battle has not yet been won. Recent data regarding the struggle for social mobility show that it is becoming increasingly difficult to move up. But we must not give up that fight. As we become an increasingly diverse nation, we must work to ensure equal opportunity for everyone . . . in housing, in education, in the job market. We must continue to talk with each other and not at each other.

One of the most effective efforts to transcend racial barriers at our university has come from our student services office. We call service the great equalizer because, when our students are out in the community building a house, teaching adults to read, or tutoring young children, they connect with one another across racial, cultural, and ethnic lines with a common goal of helping improve the lives of others.

As a lifelong teacher, I firmly believe that education is the foundation for economic success. Therefore I am pleased to report that preliminary numbers indicate that, along with our record number of students coming this fall, we will most likely have a record number of incoming African American students. And that's great news. But what's even more heartening is that, because Carolina was reintegrated more than forty years ago, we are seeing legacy students . . . the children of our black alumni starting their own academic careers at Carolina. But I also want to point out that we don't just recruit these students, we graduate them. According to the publication *Black Issues in Higher Education,* the University of South Carolina is a top producer of African Americans with baccalaureate degrees.

The University of South Carolina, our state's flagship university, has an obligation to be accessible to all the people of South Carolina, not just the wealthiest or most academically gifted but *all* the people. Again this year as I carried my Bowtie Bus Tour to each and every one of the forty-six counties in the Palmetto State, I made a point to visit many of the state's historically black high schools to encourage those students to consider enrolling at our university. To the best of my knowledge, I'm the only white president of a research university in the United States who began his academic career as faculty member in a historically black university. I fully understand that students have a large number of alternatives for higher education. But irrespective of what their goals are, please encourage your grandchildren, your nieces, your nephews, and your neighbors to study harder and be more diligent in their homework habits because the admission standards of many of our universities are on the rise. Grades and test scores that were good enough to get into Carolina yesterday are not good enough to get in tomorrow.

Just like the past forty-one years, the next forty-one years will indeed be critical ones, filled with challenges as we move into an era in which education is much more essential than it has been in the past. As we approach these decades, will we be divided, or will we stand together as one community, indivisible, working for opportunity for all? If we are to realize that dream, we must be committed to banding together—black, white, Asian, and Latino; rich and poor—through a combination of hard work, vision, and occasionally compromise. One of our greatest goals is to work toward harmonious race relations and a society where the color of a man's skin is no more predictive of what he will accomplish in his lifetime than the color of his eyes. I stand before you today knowing that, as a nation and as a community, our collective success depends on what we as individuals do. The next forty-one years will be filled with the challenges of empowering people to take responsibility, to revitalize our communities, to reinvigorate public education, to make morally sound decisions, and to broaden opportunities for all.

I'm going to give away my age by telling you about the best blues singer I have ever heard: Billie Holiday, whom we affectionately called "Lady Day." She did a lot of her singing in dimly lit, smoke-filled clubs. One of my favorite Lady Day ballads starts with these words: "You came a long way from St. Louie."

The Greater Columbia Community Relations Council has made enormous progress over the past forty-one years. And you should feel good about that as we celebrate your progress. But listen carefully to the next line of that old blues song and imagine Lady Day crooning these plaintive words: "But you still got a long way to go." On all the causes we are valiantly fighting for, in education and in economic opportunity, "we still got a long way to go."

But if we heed the words of the ancient prophet, we shall find the courage, the tenacity, and the fortitude to go the whole distance. Hearken to this timeless admonition from Isaiah: "They that wait upon the Lord shall renew their strength: they shall mount up with wings of eagles, they shall run and not be weary, they shall walk and not faint." Allow me to close by fusing the opening phrase of the Negro National Anthem with the beginning words of the song that came to characterize the life of Dr. Martin Luther King Jr.: "Lift every voice and sing 'til earth and heaven ring, we shall overcome." We shall overcome.

FIVE

Remarks upon Receiving the Greater Columbia Chamber of Commence Ambassador of the Year Award

I AM HUMBLED by your selecting me to receive this award, and I thank you for this recognition. It's indeed a privilege to be in the company of such distinguished guests and former recipients of the Greater Columbia Chamber's Ambassador of the Year Award. As the renaissance poet and Anglican priest, John Donne observed: "No man is an island . . . ; every man is a piece of the continent." Although several centuries later we have come to use inclusive language to describe that truth, I most certainly wouldn't be here today if it weren't for the support of my dear wife, Donna, my wonderful colleagues at the University of South Carolina, and so many of you throughout this state.

I'm nearing the end of my third year of Bow Tie Bus Tours during which I crisscross the state on a USC minibus, typically starting from our home at 6:45 in the morning and returning about 10:00 P.M. Last Monday I was in

St. Matthews, Moncks Corner, Charleston, and Sullivan's Island. Next Monday I'll be visiting people in Newberry, Greenville, Greenwood, and North Augusta. But no matter where I go, I tell everyone—especially prospective students and their parents—what a terrific place Columbia is. After all, USC and Columbia are a package deal. Together the two create a synergy that make Columbia and the university an unusually attractive place to come to school, to live, and to do business. When I visited Columbia during the university's presidential search, I was struck by the sense of community, not just on the Carolina campus, but throughout Columbia. There was a sense of enthusiasm and optimism, a "can do" spirit that I wanted to be a part of. I vowed that if I became Carolina's president, I would work tirelessly to ensure that the entire university would be characterized by that spirit, and work toward the goal of the Columbia and Carolina communities becoming one.

Donna and I had a very special introduction to Columbia. You may recall that during my first nineteen months as president, we lived in a home in the university neighborhood at the corner of Gregg and Pendleton streets, while the President's House was being renovated. During that time the phrase "good neighbor" took on a whole new meaning for me. I learned firsthand to respect and appreciate the meaning of that term, as well as its implicit sense of community.

There's something very special about a community— whether it's an urban neighborhood, a college campus, an entire city—that provides a source of strength and support, a wellspring of memories, a venue for debating ideas and affording a catalyst for change. But most of all, in any community, whether big or small, it's where bonds are forged and relationships are built.

Columbia is a community that is definitely on the move. Carolina is a university on the move. And with the support of the Gamecock family and the Columbia community with which it is inextricably intertwined, we will move upward and onward—together, in the words of an old favorite hymn: "All one body we." Thank you.

SIX

Remarks at the Mayor's State of the City (Columbia, South Carolina) Address

I was asked by Bob Coble, mayor of Columbia, South Carolina, to address the general public during his annual State of the City presentation on January 31, 2007.

MR. MAYOR AND FELLOW CITIZENS OF COLUMBIA. Thanks for the invitation to share with each member of the City Council several initiatives that—together with those presented by Mayor Coble and abetted by the hard work and creativity of the business community and the Richland County Council—can lead Columbia to become a nationally recognized alternative energy city. But these efforts will come to fruition only if all of us work together. Our university's central role in this endeavor is to contribute the scientific talent and research environment that will enable tomorrow's energy economy businesses to thrive. I sincerely believe that the research campus we know as Innovista will offer the physical and fiscal template for companies wishing to pursue research and development. And other firms throughout the Midlands will benefit when those discoveries lead to manufacturing opportunities.

But our university can and will do more. In February 2006 I commissioned a university-wide team to study how we could promote health on our campus. This initiative, called Healthy Carolina, led us to adopt a campuswide no smoking policy and encouraged people to modify other behaviors for their own good and that of the greater community. I truly believe that this initiative is among the very best health programs to be found in any American university. But there are other challenges before us.

Tonight I am announcing the commissioning of a group of faculty, staff, and students who will recommend to me and to our board of trustees creative ways to promote the use of alternative energy throughout our campus. I am especially interested in the utilization of fuel cell technology, whether in the form of demonstration projects—such as the one we currently have functioning in our new five-hundred-person residence hall—or, where feasible, the ability to deliver back-up or real time electricity.

We are building on our campus a station to generate enough steam to provide 80 percent of the energy required for heating and cooling all our university facilities. And here's the wonderful part: this entire plant is fueled by wood chips coming from South Carolina's renewable pine forests. I am also committed to exploring the deployment of other alternative technologies, including solar and wind technologies, because our city and our university must be known as a place where *all* energies of the future can be researched, developed, demonstrated, and deployed.

If Columbia is to be known as a future energy city, then the University of South Carolina must be known as a future energy university. Achieving this designation will require our students, faculty, and staff to be better educated about the benefits and also the barriers presented in using hydrogen and other energy forms. I will encourage the development of venues to encourage such discussion and learning across all of our academic programs.

Yet another example of innovative education that has benefited the university community as well as the greater Midlands region has been our study of the social and ethical implications of nanotechnology. This has led not only to significant federal funding, but also to our launching the Citizens' School for Nanotechnology. We will continue creative measures such as these schools and lunchtime gatherings we have branded science cafés, so that all of us may come together to learn more about the hydrogen economy and to promote Columbia's role in it. The first Citizens' School on Fuel Cell and Hydrogen Technology will be held from February 5 through March 19.

Furthermore I am committed to the principle that every new building to be constructed at the University of South Carolina will deploy at least one hydrogen fuel cell project or educational demonstration program about hydrogen or other alternative energies. I want our students, faculty, and staff to become as familiar with these "technologies of tomorrow" as if they were the technologies of today. This commitment will require considerable planning and buy-in from many people, but nothing that can transform the university comes without a price.

As you know, our Innovista buildings are already out of the ground, and once the four remaining Honeycomb dormitories are fully demolished, our new Honors College residence hall will be built on that site as yet another green, LEED certifiable residence hall. The next project to come out of the ground after that is our Gamecock baseball stadium. To illustrate my dedication to the hydrogen initiative, I have asked Rick Kelly and his staff to explore the feasibility of having hydrogen contribute to the scoreboard's power supply at the new stadium.

As I have often said, the futures of the University of South Carolina and the City of Columbia are inextricably intertwined. We continue to benefit from each other's support, and we must stimulate each other to be better than we currently are. Thank you, Mr. Mayor, and thank you, members of the City Council, for giving me the opportunity to be with you here tonight. I am deeply grateful to all of you for your continued support of our unstinting efforts to link our town and our gown.

PART THREE

The University in the State

SEVEN

The Role of Research Universities in Transforming South Carolina's Economy

AFTER BEING APPOINTED PRESIDENT of the University of South Carolina, I came to believe that by reflecting on the economic history of the Palmetto State, we might develop a better appreciation of the direction our university needed to take in the years ahead to help reshape our state's economy. Walter Edgar notes that due to the remarkably successful mercantile activity of the seventeenth century—regrettably dependent on trade in slaves and their exploitation to foster agricultural industries—Carolina was the wealthiest of the original thirteen colonies. In his classic history of our state, Professor Edgar observes that this phenomenal success was derived from an entrepreneurial, can-do spirit: "Because South Carolinians were willing to exploit whatever was available, make changes, and take chances, they were able to create a prosperous society that was the envy of British North America."

In the early years of our republic, South Carolina's dominance in trade through the Charleston seaport augured well for its future. The abundant crops of rice plantations, indigo fields, cotton plantations, and tobacco farms generated substantial wealth. Although the economy was devastated in the years after the Civil War, the Industrial Revolution later brought textile mills, providing another boon to the Carolinas. Early in the twentieth century enormous farms and hunting lodges with vast acreage drew many wealthy outsiders to this state. As they began telling their friends about the phenomenal beauty and pristine character of this state—from the marshlands and beaches of the lowcountry to the beauty of the Appalachian Mountains in the upstate, and the richly varied topography in between—tourists eventually came in droves, boosting the hospitality industry.

Today many South Carolinians reflect upon the overall trend of the past four centuries with pride and speak in glowing terms of perpetuating the wonderful traditions of those who laid the groundwork for the twenty-first century. While I appreciate how that rich history has shaped our society, I am deeply troubled by the general failure to adapt our industries to the knowledge revolution that has stimulated so much of our nation's unparalleled economic growth. Admittedly there are exceptions here and there, such as selected areas along the I-85 corridor. But those efforts pale in comparison to other parts of the country. For several decades areas such as the Silicon Valley in California, the Route 128 corridor around

Boston, and the Research Triangle in our neighboring state of North Carolina have demonstrated clearly how the sophisticated technology can dramatically affect economies far beyond the boundaries of their respective regions.

We are at a critical juncture in South Carolina's history, but we have much further to go than these nationally recognized regions because we have been tardy in exploiting the knowledge revolution. We must take steps now toward changing our business recruitment and job creation strategy or risk falling further behind the rest of the country.

In short it is imperative that we resuscitate the mentality that, in Walter Edgar's words, characterized seventeenth-century South Carolina: to "make changes and take chances." The South Carolina Competitiveness Initiative, a study recently commissioned by major stakeholders in our state's economy, contends that we can no longer compete effectively on the basis of being a low-cost place to do business.

Our rich-in-land, favorable climate, and cheap-in-labor strategy articulated so long ago provided us with a diverse industrial mix and a conscientious labor force. But that strategy simply won't work any longer. In a word South Carolina must shift its focus from low cost to high quality. If we South Carolinians wish to experience the kind of economic development of which we are capable, we must be much more aggressive and imaginative in cultivating the unending stream of intellectual property from our research universities. Our strategy to modify this state's economic development has two thrusts. First we must cultivate the talent we already have.

By harnessing South Carolina–based innovation and the brain power cultivated in our research universities, local firms will be able to improve processes, develop new products, increase sales, expand their businesses, and thus ultimately create jobs. In addition our leading-edge faculty researchers will spawn new technologies that local companies can then commercialize through start-up companies.

At the University of South Carolina we are taking measured yet bold steps toward becoming a top tier research university, in considerable measure through intensifying collaboration with our sister higher education institutions. Four years ago we announced the formation of Health Sciences South Carolina—a coalition that came to include Carolina, Clemson, and MUSC as well as the four leading teaching hospitals in the state: Palmetto Health System, Greenville Hospital System, Spartanburg Regional Hospital, and the University Hospital in Charleston. One of the primary purposes of this organization is to develop Centers of Economic Excellence, a program created by the General Assembly with the goal of attracting to South Carolina the world's most talented researchers—those who are working to create the superstar technologies of tomorrow.

This visionary initiative, also known as the Endowed Chairs Program, leverages state and private funds along with university-based research to drive economic growth. These centers house research in targeted industries with the greatest promise to create high-skill, high-paying jobs. State funds for the program come from S.C. Education Lottery proceeds and must be matched dollar for dollar with nonstate monies from corporations, foundations, or private donors. This model has created a magnet for private-sector investment South Carolina.

The second thrust of our new strategy is this: as we work with other institutions within our state's boundaries, we must simultaneously recruit nationally eminent scientists to our research universities and at the same time attract, retain, and grow a critical mass of forward-thinking, knowledge-based companies from across the nation and around the world.

While it is true that research universities have as one of their primary missions the creation of knowledge and charting previously unmapped intellectual terrain, it is imperative that these endeavors not be restricted to faculty, staff, and students of research universities. Baccalaureate institutions, community colleges, and technical schools must be intimately involved in the activity of translating these scientific discoveries if we are to achieve the economic transformation we so desperately need. Technical school faculty and students at present are not generally involved in these initiatives. Their relative lack of involvement comes from two sources: in many research universities an intellectual snobbery that assumes that the only academics who are capable of embarking on such initiatives and leading them are research university faculty. This is palpably untrue, and such arrogance needs to be laid to rest.

As we cast a wider net for scholarly involvement, it would be singularly inappropriate not to solicit aggressively the involvement of technical school faculty, staff, and students. Shortly after becoming president of Carolina, I suggested that we include the Midlands Technical College in our Small Business Incubator Program. Every fall we have a ceremony in which we celebrate the graduation of one of our student-led initiatives from this program. Not only do we feature graduates of our university, but recently two Midlands Tech students, working with their faculty, developed two start-up businesses growing out of their intellectual property and have formed corporations to commercialize their respective discoveries. This is but one facet of our efforts to reach out to our technical college colleagues.

All these efforts demonstrate unequivocally the University of South Carolina's commitment to recruiting individual companies through collaborative efforts involving the commercial, governmental, and educational sectors. But if initiatives such as these are to bear fruit, public research universities must dip deeper into the innovation stream, and—to extend the metaphor—push harder to build bridges between our educational programs and technological innovations on one shore and across that stream to what knowledge-driven businesses need.

As those of us in the public sector—at technical schools as well as research universities—join forces with those of you in the private sector, we can create an environment rife with economic activity that makes this a place where the brightest and best want to live. That will be a place where people are talking about great school systems, terrific universities, and meaningful career opportunities; and a place where responsible government is working hand in hand with its taxpayers to preserve our remarkable natural resources for future generations.

The development of the Innovista—which is designed to support existing South Carolina–based innovation as well as attract industries from all over the country and around the world—will be greatly enhanced for the increased collaboration among our institutions of higher education through initiatives such as the Endowed Chairs Program and our Small Business Incubator Program, the creation of Health Sciences South Carolina, the impact of the South Carolina Competitive Initiative, and the launching of the Bridge Program: all these are watershed events for us. We now have a road map to guide us in making changes that will bring true prosperity to our state.

Only one question remains: Are South Carolinians ready to embrace this new model of economic development? If we are all committed to making these changes in a unified fashion, we will not fail. The challenge before us is monumental, and in several respects our near term prospects are formidable. But I truly believe that if we find ways to coordinate our resources to elevate the quality of research and teaching in all South Carolina institutions of higher education—and at the same time invest in the high-tech and knowledge-revolution industries that

are capable of transforming the economy of this state—
we shall accomplish far more than if we work in splendid
isolation from one another or if we persist in pouring
new wine in old bottles. I pray that you will join me as we
usher in a new day for South Carolina.

EIGHT

The Transformation of Research and Education in the Health Professions at the University of South Carolina

DURING THE PAST SIX YEARS, there has been a remarkable transformation of research and education in the School of Medicine and the other health professions schools—specifically nursing, pharmacy, public health, and social work—at the University of South Carolina. In this chapter I explain how these changes were effected while we have continued to support our original mission.

The Context in which the USC School of Medicine Was Founded

Economist Monica Noether contends that the American Medical Association's relaxation of policies that restricted the supply of physicians in the mid-1960s allowed "both federal and state government" to enact "funding programs to encourage expansion of existing medical schools and the creation of new ones."[1] In response to this accommodation, "twenty-five new medical schools were funded during the decade of the 1970s."[2] The University of South

Carolina School of Medicine is one of five schools created in the mid-1970s under the aegis of the Teague-Cranston Act.[3] All were built on Veterans Administration hospital campuses in conjunction with public universities, in order to train physicians for medically underserved areas and to benefit "veterans and their families."[4] The faculty who were recruited for these schools contended that, because their primary purpose was to prepare doctors for general medical practice, basic and clinical research was marginal to their mission. They reasoned that the combination of federal largesse and support from their respective state legislatures did not require them to secure substantial external support for their research, and they assumed that a modicum of scholarly activity was adequate.

The discussion surrounding the passage of the Teague-Cranston Act reflected a desire to present a corrective to the evolution of academic medical centers in the post–World War II era: "Research and the practice of the medical and surgical specialties that were built upon the translation of research into patient care, created complex enterprises that became institutions unto themselves, increasingly removed from the patients and the communities in which they lived."[5] Generally the schools founded during the 1970s espoused the importance not only of training physicians for "family practice," but also of addressing the "medical care needs of the community as a whole."[6]

The ancestor of the Medical University of South Carolina (MUSC)—the Medical College of South Carolina

—was founded in 1824. By the time the USC School of Medicine was founded, MUSC was a large academic health center with its own teaching hospital and a robust program of externally funded research. There was considerable political opposition within the state regarding the creation of a second publicly funded medical school, but USC—like the other Teague-Cranston schools—appealed to the need for more primary care practitioners in a heavily rural state and won the day.

The Need for Creating a Division of Health Sciences

When I was appointed president of USC in 2002, the dean of the School of Medicine was also vice president for clinical affairs and reported to the president. All the other health professions deans reported to the provost. The board of trustees—based on advice from a committee, faculty, administrators, and external consultants—finalized a proposal in 2000 to amalgamate these five colleges into the Division of Health Sciences reporting directly to one person. It was hoped that this change would stimulate collaboration across these entities and enhance their academic stature. But in the intervening years no progress had been made in implementing this recommendation.

Especially in recent years, virtually every academic medical health center has professed a strong commitment to scientific collaboration and shared teaching responsibility among the health professions schools. The encouragement by the NIH and NSF for transdisciplinary research—as well as the demonstrable and substantial benefits of such scholarship and pedagogy—certainly warranted its creation. We desperately needed, in the words of Henry Rosovsky, the "lowering [of] internal barriers."[7] However, if there was to be substantial change in the relations among these schools, it was imperative that all the deans and at least a high proportion of faculty buy into the process. Given the meager evidence of scientific collaboration among the health professions schools on our campus, it seemed prudent to meet with a representative faculty group and the deans of the respective entities to explore the proposal for a Division of Health Sciences. These conversations began in earnest in the late fall of 2002.

Ramping Up the Infrastructure for IT and the Office of Sponsored Research (OSR)

As these discussions progressed about the need for elevating the academic reputation of the university in general and the health sciences in particular. it was abundantly obvious to all participants that a critical element was a substantial surge in grant and contract activity. However, a survey of both our IT systems and OSR functions indicated these units were not geared up to handle such an increase. When I arrived at USC, 100 percent of all OSR forms were filled out manually, with paper being sent from one office to another. This archaic process not only consumed a lot of time (and trees) but presented needless hurdles whose obsolescence dampened the entrepreneurial instincts of the faculty. They pointed out that, if we were to achieve the lofty goals for academic excellence we had articulated, we needed what an NSF advisory panel on cyberinfrastructure as a layer on which "scientific and engineering research and education environments could be built."[8] Our faculty sentiments were later corroborated by the NSF in its "first-ever analysis of academe's information technology infrastructure," which concluded that more extensive and ever faster computer networks are essential to doctoral institutions.[9] We had accumulated a reserve of Indirect Cost (IDC) funds in our OSR and decided to provide several million dollars from this fund to enhance our IT capability, to increase the size of our OSR staff, and to facilitate their capacity to submit and track electronically all research proposals and all awarded grants and contracts. Our assumption was that this would stimulate a marked escalation of grants and contract proposals and that the resultant increase in IDC recoveries would enable us to recoup this investment. Our prediction proved to be warranted.

In order to get the Division of Health Sciences up and running and at the same time improve the OSR infrastructure, we created the position of vice president for research and health sciences in the spring of 2003. Having all five health sciences deans report to this VP seemed wise, but because we did not own a teaching hospital— at least in the near term—this person could concomitantly guide the needed improvement of the OSR. A national search that summer and fall resulted in Harris Pastides being appointed VP in December 2003. Within a few months the electronic system was launched, and by the spring of 2005 it was fully operational.

Investing in Faculty Expansion

The drive to expand our research enterprise also was abetted mightily by two faculty hiring plans. The first, launched by Provost Jerry Odom in the fall of 2003, is the Faculty Excellence Initiative (FEI), stimulated by his calculation that over the next five years about one-third of our full-time faculty (N=350) would be retiring. Given our plans to foster the gradual growth of the student body and at the same time reduce the student:faculty ratio, the provost recommended that we add 150 tenure/tenure-track positions over the next six years—an average of 25 per year. That, plus replacement, would mean recruiting 500 new faculty over a period of several years. We dedicated $2 million from tuition revenues for each of the first two years (FY04 and FY05) for this program. Then in the spring of 2005 we persuaded our state legislature to give us 4 million recurring dollars in FY06, and another 4.8 million in FY07, for a total of $8.8 million.

Also in the fall of 2003 we launched a quite different initiative: the Centenary Plan (CP), so named because over a six-year period we would add one hundred full-time research faculty. These faculty are not offered tenure/tenure-track positions and are given three-year contracts with the following terms: for the first two years, 50 percent of a CP professor's salary is paid by the vice president for research; in the third year that percentage is reduced to 25. The balance of the professor's salary support comes from his or her unit and/or extramural funding. The program is designed to establish clearly defined economic incentives to secure external research support. It is expected that from the fourth year onward, grant and contract revenues and support from the respective units will cover 100 percent of the CP faculty member's salary, or that person will leave. All the new faculty—under both the FEI and CP initiatives—have been recruited from universities in which the expectation for an entrepreneurial spirit and a high level of scholarly productivity —as well as dedication to teaching—is universal. Of the sixteen current academic deans, only one was here when I was named as president. Most of the credit for the remarkably successful faculty recruitment goes to the new deans, whose commitments to scholarly excellence and fund-raising were immediately apparent.

The Return on the Investment

The gamble was more effective than we dared to dream, and the results greatly exceeded our expectations. The year before I came to USC, external grant and contract awards (not counting any portion of the annual state legislative appropriation as research funding) totaled $109 million. At the end of my first year (FY03), it was $131 million; the next year it was $149 million, a year later $166 million, at the end of the fourth year $173 million, and at the end of the fifth year (FY07) more than $185 million—an increase of 70 percent. We have data for only the first eight months of FY08, but our year-over-year comparisons show that we are up 20 percent in extramural awards over the first eight months of FY07. Even if we were to experience a year-over-year decline in the last four months of FY08, we are very likely to exceed

$200 million—nearly doubling extramural funding in six years!

For the health professions schools the growth has been even more impressive than for the university as a whole. NIH awards grew from $7.4 million in FY02 to $21.9 million for FY07, very nearly a threefold increase. Awards from all other sources went from $35.8 million in FY02 to $55.3 million in FY07, a nearly 54 percent increase. The extraordinary success of the faculty in the Division of Health Sciences resulted in a total five-year growth from $43.2 million to $77.2 million (more than 78 percent), nearly doubling during a period of intense competition and gradual plateauing of NIH funding. The substantial improvements in the functioning of the research infrastructure—to say nothing of the early and widespread success in securing grants and contracts, to which the newly recruited deans and faculty contributed substantially—palpably lifted morale throughout the university.

The Integration of Pharmacy Schools

As our research portfolio grew, we launched two ambitious initiatives through the Division of Health Sciences designed to increase our collective efforts by a quantum leap, principally by collaborating closely with other institutions. Raymond Greenberg, president of the Medical University of South Carolina (MUSC), and I had been friends for decades before I became president at USC. From the very outset, we began exploring ways in which our institutions might work together more closely.

During my first year, observing that each of us had a dean of the College of Pharmacy who was retiring, we reasoned that it would be propitious to explore the possibility of integrating these colleges. In the fall of 2003, we launched discussions on our respective campuses. A committee composed of faculty from each school met to design a common curriculum, centralized admissions process, and a mutually acceptable governance structure. After extensive discussions and thoughtful analysis of how synergies across our institutional boundaries would enable us to achieve more together than we could separately, the USC and MUSC boards of trustees approved the creation of a new entity in the fall of 2004: the South Carolina College of Pharmacy (SCCP).

The plan Dr. Greenberg and I presented to our respective schools included the establishment of three SCCP campuses. One on the MUSC campus in Charleston, one on the USC campus in Columbia one hundred miles north, and the third on the campus of the Greenville Hospital System (GHS) another hundred miles north. In January 2005 the GHS pledged $5 million to support pharmacy education on their campus, in addition to building an education building to accommodate classrooms and offices for the faculty. That building will open in the fall of 2008. Joseph DiPiro was hired as executive dean of SCCP in May 2005, and in June 2006 precandidate status for the first college of pharmacy in the United States to emerge from previously separate accredited colleges of pharmacy was granted by the American Council of Pharmacy Education (ACPE). In August 2006 we admitted 190 students to the first SCCP class, and in June 2007 we achieved candidate status from ACPE.

The Formation of Health Sciences South Carolina (HSSC)

In parallel with the emergence of SCCP, we joined forces with MUSC, its teaching hospital, and the two USC affiliate hospitals—neither of which was recognized at that time as a university medical center—to organize another initiative. If USC and MUSC wished to enlarge our clinical research capability, we felt it was imperative that we develop a more formal, structured relationship with the four largest teaching hospitals in the state. But rather than focusing exclusively on what would be beneficial only to USC, in the spring of 2003 we began exploring ways in which all of our research universities could collaborate with these hospitals. Steven Wartman has pointed out the heightened sensitivity among university leaders to the fact that the "highly competitive national and international environment . . . renders internal dissonance within an institution a drag on resources, spirit, and intellectual creativity. Simply put, most institutions are finding it increasingly difficult and costly to have some of their key components working at cross purposes."[10] The appropriateness of this observation was apparent to us as we surveyed other universities and witnessed the inhibiting effect of competition among medical centers on their ability to reach their full potential.

As the benefits of synergy among all entities became increasingly evident, we expanded our consortium in the spring of 2004 and created a 501 (c) (3) corporation (HSSC), which consists of the only two medical schools in the state, all three research universities (USC, MUSC, and Clemson), and the four largest teaching hospitals (Greenville Hospital System, Palmetto Health System, Spartanburg Regional Hospital, and the University Hospital at MUSC). The mission of HSSC is to conduct health sciences research to improve health status, education, workforce development, and economic well-being for all South Carolinians. The fact that the CEOs of the respective entities are the only members of the board of directors has greatly enhanced our ability to collaborate across institutional boundaries.

In order to facilitate the development of HSSC programs, each of the three nonuniversity hospitals agreed to contribute $2 million per year to the collective budget, and each university agreed to contribute $1 million in cash per year from discretionary funds, for a total of $9 million annually. In addition each university contributes another $1 million per year dedicated to faculty and facility infrastructure, making a grand total of $12 million annually. To the best of our knowledge, this is the only entity in the United States to pool the resources of all research universities and teaching hospitals statewide, each contributing substantial fiscal support from their respective budgets *exclusive of* revenues from grants and contracts as well as state support.

In September 2007 we hired Jay Moskowitz as president of HSSC. He also serves as director of the Center for Healthcare Quality and occupies an endowed chair at USC with joint appointments at MUSC and Clemson. Although it is premature to predict fully the success of HSSC, we believe that—given our collective ability to secure research funds (which currently total more than $500 million annually) and additionally to establish a multimillion dollar annual operating budget—these accomplishments are truly harbingers of increasingly productive research and the improved health status of South Carolinians in the years to come.

Shortly after the establishment of HSSC, we submitted a proposal to the Duke Endowment to launch research initiatives addressing patient safety, clinical effectiveness, and health care quality—goals that are highly congruent with the HSSC mission. With respect to clinical effectiveness and health care quality, we are developing outreach programs targeting communities that are adjacent to our academic medical centers.[11] Commenting on the Duke Endowment's $21 million grant enabling us to advance our research in these areas, Institute of Medicine president Fineberg said in a press release, "This pacesetting gift from The Duke Endowment will help propel South Carolina into the forefront of research on patient safety, clinical effectiveness, and quality of health care. . . . I salute the leaders of The Duke Endowment and in the State of South Carolina for an enterprise that can improve the lives of millions and become a model for the nation." At the announcement of this award, a former dean of the Duke University Medical School (who is also a member of the Duke Endowment board of directors) noted the uniqueness of having 100 percent of the medical schools and teaching hospitals in one state creating an entity, such as HSSC, dedicated to such systemic coherence.

In parallel with expanding the IT infrastructure at USC, we have been developing an IT network linking all three research universities. It will eventually connect all HSSC institutions and provide a functional, electronic clinical trials network and a universal IRB. Even now institutional human subjects review for a project being conducted at each partner site requires only one review. This is tangible evidence of our willingness to cede local authority for the benefit of statewide clinical research. If we can achieve a fully integrated IT network, the opportunities for clinical and epidemiological research (as well as other types of research) are greatly enhanced. Given the huge cost of establishing such a network, we requested and received $4.5 million from the state legislature to seed the integration of these IT systems. We are now tied into the National LambdaRail and—in parallel with our colleagues elsewhere—are laying the "foundation for the next-generation networks needed to support large-scale research, education outreach, public/private partnerships, and new models of collaboration while providing the requisite IT infrastructure vital to economic development."[12] While we are grateful that our request to the state legislature was approved, we are acutely aware that each of our institutions will have to provide substantial supplements to that appropriation to achieve such an ambitious goal.

The Importance of Remaining True to Our Mission while Transforming Health Care Research and Education

In sum, over the past six years, the USC medical school has moved from a position of relative insularity from the other colleges within the university—conducting little extramural research and regarding its relationship with its teaching hospitals as distal associated institutions—to a position of full integration into the Division of Health Sciences, very significant growth in externally funded research, and working more closely than ever before with its two teaching hospitals—one of which recently secured designation as a university health center. These results are particularly noteworthy given the inherent propensity of organizations to resist change. A survey of 127 U.S. academic health centers (to which 65 responded) indicated that "most organizations did not wish to change the fundamental nature of their identities."[13] Thus the modification of our academic culture is particularly noteworthy.

However, as we have elevated considerably our commitment to biomedical and health care research, we have not neglected the family medicine and community-based model on which we were founded. Indeed, during the 1990s we opened a family medicine clinic in a rural community, and four years ago we opened a similar clinic in yet another rural community. These two rural programs build on the aspirations of the founding faculty not only by serving the health care needs of local residents but also by providing settings through which our medical and nursing students as well as residents may rotate as they consider practicing in underserved communities. We have also continued to remain true to the purpose of preparing graduates for practice in primary care. Over the past ten years, an average of 75 percent of each graduating class has enters entered primary care, and of those 60 percent remain in South Carolina.

The opportunities before us are truly extraordinary. We hope that the model of interinstitutional collaboration we are developing throughout our region will be thought worthy of emulation elsewhere. Nearly a decade ago, Samuel Thier and Nannerl Keohane observed: "The future of academic health centers rests on all of us."[14] The urgency of their admonition is timeless, even though such institutions have continued to evolve in the years since then. Unless we are more creative and tenacious in transcending university and hospital organizational structures, we run the risk of jeopardizing our collective future.

NOTES

1. Monica Noether, "The Effect of Government Policy Change on the Supply of Physicians," *Journal of Law and Economics* 29 (October 1986): 234.

2. Robert Ebert, "The Medical School Revisited," *Health Affairs* 4 (Summer 1985): 55.

3. Public Law 92-541 (October 24, 1972; H.JRes 748).

4. H.R. 2125IH (May 15, 2003).

5. T. W. Langitt, "Values in Health Care and Health Professions Education," *Proceedings of the American Philosophical Society* 141 (September 1999): 401.

6. Patricia West and Wilmer Coggins, *A Special Kind of Doctor* (Tuscaloosa: University of Alabama Press, 2004).

7. Henry Rosovsky, "No Ivory Tower: University and Society in the Twenty-first Century," in *As the Walls of Academia Are Tumbling Down*, edited by Luc E. Weber and Werner Z. Hirsch (Paris: Economica, 2002), 27.

8. National Science Foundation, *Revolutionizing Science and Engineering through Cyberinfrastructure: Report of the NSF Blue Ribbon Advisory Panel on Cyberinfrastructure*, January 2003, p. 5. www.cisc.nsf.gov/sci/reports/toc.cfm

9. InfoBrief, "Universities Continue to Expand Their Research Space with the Largest Increase since 1988, Data Reported for Networking Capacity," NSF 05-114 (June 2005).

10. Steven A. Wartman, AAHC Report from the President, August 9, 2007.

11. Thomas Plochg, Diana Delnoij, and Nick Klazinga, "Linking Up with the Community: A Fertile Strategy for a University Hospital?" *International Journal of Integrated Care* 6 (January–March 2006): 1–15.

12. Larry Conrad and Veronica Sarjeant, "Leveraging National LambdaRail: The Road to RDN," *Educause Review* 40 (July/August 2005): 77.

13. Alice Adams, "Organizational Identity in Academic Health Centers" Ph.D. diss., University of Alabama at Birmingham, 2004. Abstract in *Dissertation Abstracts International*, publ. nr. AAT 3149757.

14. Samuel Thier and Nannerl Keohane, "How Can We Assure the Survival of Academic Health Centers?" *Chronicle of Higher Education*, March 13, 1998.

NINE

Fully Fund the
Endowed Chairs Program
It's a Smart Investment in South Carolina's Future

JIM BARKER, PRESIDENT, CLEMSON UNIVERSITY

RAY GREENBERG, PRESIDENT,
MEDICAL UNIVERSITY OF SOUTH CAROLINA

ANDREW SORENSEN, PRESIDENT,
UNIVERSITY OF SOUTH CAROLINA

IMAGINE IF THE BUSINESS WORLD'S "NEXT BIG THING"—
the next Microsoft or Genentech—were headquartered
in South Carolina. Think of the high-paying jobs—in
R&D, engineering, and human resources—that such a
company would create here and the effect that inflow of
payroll, capital investment, and tax revenue would have
on our economy. How do we make this happen?

Five years ago the General Assembly created a program
designed to attract to South Carolina the world's most
talented researchers—those who are, in fact, working
to create the superstar technologies of tomorrow. This
visionary initiative, the Centers of Economic Excellence

Program (also known as the Endowed Chairs Program) leverages state and private funds along with university-based research to drive economic growth.

To date, the program has brought thirteen world-class scientists, or "endowed chairs," to our state's universities. It has also established thirty Centers of Economic Excellence in research areas such as nanotechnology, health sciences, future fuels, energy alternatives, automotive engineering, and advanced fibers. These centers house research in targeted industries with the greatest promise to create high-skill, high-paying jobs. State funds for the program come from S.C. Education Lottery proceeds and must be matched dollar-for-dollar with nonstate monies from corporations, foundations, or private donors. This model has created a magnet for private-sector investment in South Carolina.

The state's three research universities—Clemson University, the University of South Carolina, and the Medical University of South Carolina—are using the program to benefit our state. In addition to increased research collaboration among the three institutions, we are now able to get the attention of the world's best scientists and graduate students.

As an example, BMW, Michelin, Timken, and other South Carolina companies recognize the value of the research now happening in the state. They've tapped into those capabilities and have stepped up to fund endowed chairs. World-class scientists recruited under the program are now generating technology that these and other companies can commercialize to create new products, improve processes, increase sales, and ultimately create jobs.

The Centers of Economic Excellence Program is helping us attract new companies to South Carolina—which could produce an immediate pay-off for the state in jobs and investment—based on the value of research and innovation happening here. What's more, the program is also beginning to create spin-off companies from university research in high-growth, high-wage industries.

South Carolina's students also benefit from the program. Increasing the level of training we can provide lets us keep our best and brightest at home, helping to end our talent export. In addition the presence of top researchers via the Endowed Chairs Program helps attract top-flight students from other states. Statistics show that many of these bright minds will remain in South Carolina following graduation. Together, these in-state and out-of-state students can become our next generation of innovators.

South Carolina's political leadership should be commended for creating and supporting the Centers of Economic Excellence Program during the last five years. Continuing to fund this effort fully must be a high priority. Changing course would be devastating, costing us precious momentum in our battle to gain ground toward greater success in the knowledge economy.

We encourage our state's leaders not to look at funding the Endowed Chairs Program as an appropriation, but rather as an investment—a smart investment that will fuel innovation, enhance economic opportunity, and lead to a stronger South Carolina.

PART FOUR

The University in the World

TEN

∽

The Principal Challenges to Public Higher Education in the United States

THERE ARE MANY STRIKING SIMILARITIES in the challenges we face not only north and south of the Canada-U.S. border, but also in Australia, Asia, and the United Kingdom. In the interest of brevity, I shall focus on just a few of the numerous challenges that fall under the rubric of parochialism.

1

The first challenge is the imperative to transcend disciplinary boundaries. During the thirty-eight years I have served as a university professor and administrator, there has been a noticeable shift in the orientation of the professoriat away from fealty to their home institutions, especially as they seek and receive tenure, to loyalty to their respective disciplines. It is my conviction that this shift has increased dramatically over the past couple of decades.

When I began my professorial career, faculty often spoke warmly of devotion to their university. Although they often complained about subpar salaries, minimal office space, and invariably inadequate parking, even among the perennial malcontents, there was grudging admiration for the traditions that the institution preserved and for the heritage the faculty felt privileged to continue—even if their enthusiasm could hardly be described as unabated.

Particularly in our research universities, as the standards for promotion and tenure have risen, exhibited by the increased emphasis on scholarly productivity— whether manifested in externally funded research and resultant publications in refereed journals or participation in juried competitions or favorable reviews of one's scholarly work—we have, perhaps unwittingly, fostered allegiance to peers within the discipline but at other institutions. As we emphasize the importance of raising the bar in search of a more prominent place in the academic landscape, in part by employing professors at peer and peer-aspirant universities to judge our own faculty, we have asserted in at least one respect that orientation to divisions within the academy supersedes allegiance to any given institution.

This phenomenon has a direct analogue among those Peter Drucker has designated "knowledge workers" in corporations. He observes, "Communities of practice reaching across corporate boundaries are often stronger than bonds with a particular company." In the preceding sentence substituting the word "institutional" for "corporate" and "university" for "company" succinctly conveys the current situation in the academy. Indeed a recent conference of scholars across the life sciences, physical sciences, and engineering fields was convened in response to a congressional directive to the NIH asking them "to discuss what needs to be done to encourage progress in the physical sciences that will provide support and underpinning for future advances in the life sciences." Many of the participants opined that the "narrow reward system" and "the rigid departmental boundaries in academia devalue the contributions that faculty make to fields outside their discipline." It is supremely ironic that this perception is widespread at exactly the same time that the NIH and NSF have issued clear guidelines that encourage multidisciplinary and interinstitutional proposals.

2

This propensity to focus within disciplines provides a segue to our second challenge: to transcend institutional and political boundaries. In virtually each of the fifty states in the American Republic, support for institutions of higher education from our respective legislative bodies has declined substantially over the past few years. Nicholas Barr has observed that in some jurisdictions governments have recognized that research-intensive universities stimulate economic development and consequently have increased public funding of these institutions.[1] And Ronald Daniels and Michael Trebilcock correctly note that several states increased their funding between 1995 and 2001.[2] However, over the past three or four years, this situation has changed considerably. For the university over which I preside, the appropriations from our state legislature accounted for 38 percent of all university revenues in the year 2000. Four years later that had decreased by more than one-third to 24 percent, parallel to the situation in Australia described by Stephen Parker[3] and the United Kingdom as described by Bahram Bekhradnia.[4]

At a meeting two weeks ago of presidents of U.S. public universities, several commented that the support of their respective legislatures had fallen below 10 percent, with many noting draconian cuts over the past several years. Indeed, the University of Virginia now receives 8 percent of its annual budget from its state legislature. Daniels and Trebilcock lament the fact that in 2001 government funds account for 47.8 percent of revenues of Ontario universities, "the lowest in Canada,"[5] but exactly twice the proportion in my university and about six times greater than the University of Virginia. Although a few states, including my own, are facing the prospect of modest increases in support of higher education for the next fiscal year, in most instances the magnitude of the increments will barely offset the rate of inflation and surely will not redress the substantial cuts we have experienced recently.

Among the several reasons for us to transcend our respective institutional and political boundaries in finding ways to increase both our efficiency and effectiveness are the following:

• In a few instances, although I think the impact is often exaggerated, we can achieve economies of scale in integration of programs and initiatives. For example in a previous position a sister university and ours, independently of one another, were negotiating for acquisition of computer hardware and software that totaled millions of dollars annually. Because we were one, rather than two compelling parties, we saved $11 million in the first year of the contract.

+ To my mind a much more important consequence of transcending institutional boundaries is the synergy of scholarly endeavors that it precipitates. If the activities of faculty and staff working together across these boundaries are coordinated and territorial sensibilities are diminished, we can be enormously more effective in competing for funding and elevating scholarly productivity. This is truly a situation in which the whole can be enormously greater than the sum of its parts. Although there are numerous problems in cross-institutional collaboration—such as "conflicting policies on intellectual property or procedures for involving human subjects in research," these hurdles can be overcome. One example is the Network for Earthquake Engineering Simulation grid, which although in a "prototype phase" holds the promise to "be as good as face-to-face communication."

+ A serendipitous benefit of transcending these boundaries is that faculty and staff morale is enhanced by the sincere belief that the resources of the institution are being used more effectively.

If more bang for the buck is actually delivered and the faculty has irrefutable evidence that its level of productivity has risen as a consequence, the effect on its morale is bound to be salubrious.

3

The third challenge is to transcend barriers of race and class in our search for academic excellence, which is a desired outcome of transcending disciplines as well as institutional and political boundaries. There is an inevitable tension between the drive to enhance an institution's academic reputation on the one hand and, on the other hand, providing access to those who have not been privileged to acquire adequate preparation for university education. It is my firm belief that those two goals need not be mutually exclusive. In fact I submit that we have a moral responsibility to provide access to our very best institutions to families who are unable to afford the economic, pedagogic, and psychological support to prepare their children for university work. In Barr's words, "It is immoral if people with the aptitudes and desire are denied access if they cannot afford it."[6] More than thirty years ago, Martin Trow urged us—as we made the transition from elite to mass higher education—to balance considerations of equity and access with maintaining excellence.[7] Ruth Hayhoe and Qiang Zha offer compelling evidence from Taiwan that this balance can be achieved,[8] which I can corroborate from my own experience in Taiwan overseeing a graduate program sponsored by their Ministry of Health.

Daniels and Trebilcock appropriately recommend "government intervention . . . to ensure equality of opportunity for all students."[9] But unless we can develop policies to dampen the effect of the regressive transfer caused by the use of general tax revenues to fund higher education —a phenomenon noted by Bruce Chapman and David Greenaway, among others[10]—we shall continue to discriminate against students from low-income families. Thus Barr's intriguing analysis of recent developments in the United Kingdom to overcome these disparities merit emulation and special consideration on this side of the Atlantic.[11]

In virtually all public universities in the United States, we continue to raise tuition at a rate greater than inflation to offset cuts in legislative appropriations. This, however, merely exacerbates the regressiveness of government funding and, as Daniels and Trebilcock point out, "reduces the opportunity of less well-off individuals to benefit from post-secondary education."[12] In many states south of the Canadian border we have superimposed yet another layer of regressive transfer on top of the two created by government funding and student fees. A number of our universities derive huge economic benefit from lottery revenues, to which the poor and near-poor contribute at a disproportionately high level.

4

The fourth challenge is to foster a truly entrepreneurial culture within the academy without compromising our institutional integrity. As we embark on this path, we must maintain our passionate commitment to open intellectual inquiry and resist what my late colleague "Kit" Lasch characterized in *The Revolt of the Elites* as "the university's assimilation into the corporate order."[13] Or in Bekhradnia's formulation, the university must be a moral conscience for our society.[14] While it is absolutely essential to assert that the fiscal tail cannot be allowed to wag the academic dog, we must not be indifferent to the societal needs that funding agencies address. In the United States, for example, the National Institutes of Health has provided exponential increases in funding for research into HIV infection and AIDS. It would be indefensible for a university with faculty whose scholarly interests were in this field to say, "We refuse to do HIV research for the sole reason that we don't want the NIH suggesting that we should pursue their priorities."

The conundrum facing us is to determine how our research universities might dip deeper into the innovation stream, and—to extend the metaphor—simultaneously build bridges between our educational programs and technological innovations on one shore, and across that stream to what knowledge-driven businesses need. As corporations cut back on research and development done in-house, looking for external sources of innovation and breakthrough developments, we may respond to some of their overtures without compromising the integrity of our mission. Given our desperate need to cultivate other sources of funding, it is imperative that we become more aggressive in generating revenues from the intellectual property of our faculty—and in the process create high quality jobs for our graduates. Given the impetus at research universities around the globe to exploit the knowledge revolution, Bekhradnia offered—although tongue-in-cheek—a formula for a university desirous of establishing a unique niche in the academy: stimulate the development of an economy that is not driven by the knowledge revolution.[15] But irrespective of the role one believes is appropriate for our institutions in this increasingly global economy, there is a universal demand for upward social mobility that our students expect their universities to facilitate.

The challenges before us are monumental, and in several respects our near term prospects are formidable. To borrow a theme from Jim Collins's best-selling book, we need a "good-to-great transformation." But Collins warns that such transformations "never happened in one fell swoop. Like pushing on a giant, heavy fly wheel, it takes a lot of effort to get the thing moving at all, but with persistent pushing in a consistent direction over a long period of time, the fly wheel builds momentum eventually hitting a point of breakthrough."[16]

I truly believe that if we find ways to transcend academic disciplines, institutional and political boundaries, and race and class barriers in order to elevate the quality of research and teaching in all public universities and at the same time invest in the knowledge-revolution-driven industries that are capable of transforming the economy of our respective regions, we shall move from good to great universities and in the process accomplish far more than if we work in splendid isolation from one another, or if we persist in pouring new wine into old bottles.

Quite frankly, however, success will not occur without a long-term commitment from government, business, and education. As pointed out by Harvard professor Michael Porter, who has served as our principal consultant on a program to foster public-private partnerships between universities and knowledge-revolution-driven industries, the race we are in is not a sprint; it's a marathon.[17] The momentum required to meet in a sustained fashion the challenges I have described will be achieved only if we are dedicated to the synergy of purpose that commitment to coherence will yield. However, we will be highly success-ful only if, in concert with our sister institutions, we are able to serve as a driving force in shaping higher educa-tion in North America for the twenty-first century.

NOTES

1. Nicholas Barr, "Higher Education Funding," in *Taking Public Universities Seriously*, edited by Frank Iacobucci and Carolyn Tuohy, 441–75 (Toronto: University of Toronto Press, 2005).

2. Ronald Daniels and Michael Trebilcock, "Towards a New Compact in University Education in Toronto," in ibid., 87–118.

3. Stephen Parker, "Australian Education: Crossroads or Crisis?" in ibid., 26–37.

4. Bahram Bekhradnia, "Diverse Challenges, Diverse Solu-tions," in ibid., 38–43.

5. Daniels and Trebilcock, "Towards a New Compact."

6. Barr, "Higher Education Funding."

7. Martin Trow, *Problems in the Transition from Elite to Mass Higher Education* (New York: Carnegie Commission on Higher Education, 1973).

8. Ruth Hayhoe and Qiang Zha, "The Role of Public Universities in the Move to Mass Higher Education," in *Taking Public Universities Seriously*, 5–25.

9. Daniels and Trebilcock, "Towards a New Compact."

10. Bruce Chapman and David Greenaway, "Learning to Live with Loans? Policy Transfer and Funding of Higher Education" (paper, Internationalism and Policy Transfer Conference, Tulane University, 2003).

11. Barr, "Higher Education Funding."

12. Daniels and Trebilcock, "Towards a New Compact."

13. Christopher Lasch, *The Revolt of the Elites* (New York: Norton, 1995).

14. Bekhradnia, "Diverse Challenges."

15. Ibid.

16. James C. Collins, *Good to Great: Why Some Companies Make the Leap—and Others Don't* (New York: HarperBusiness, 2001).

17. Michael Porter, quoted in "Governor Sanford Attends Unveiling of Monitor Report," *Columbia State*, December 9, 2003.

ELEVEN

Bridging the Gap between Academic Health Centers and the Rest of the Academy

IN 1959 THE ENGLISH PHYSICIST and novelist C. P. Snow delivered the Rede Lecture at the University of Cambridge and titled it "Between Two Cultures."[1] In it he lamented the chasm between the basic sciences and the humanities. He knew the divide well, because he traversed it all his professional life—doing physics and writing novels. During my four decade career as a professor in medicine and the humanities, a public health dean, then a medical center administrator, and successively president in two comprehensive research universities, I have observed another chasm: it's between academic health centers and the rest of the institutions in which they are housed.

Perhaps the most important factor contributing to this gap, which has grown exponentially in the intervening decades, is the increasing atomization of knowledge and the concomitant proliferation of subdisciplines and subspecialties. A salient example of what is happening is the supremely ironic transmogrification of the general practice of medicine to a specialty: family medicine. To compound the irony, many of its practitioners refer to themselves as subspecialists within family medicine.

An unintended, but nonetheless regrettable, consequence of this proliferation is that it serves to inhibit dialogue among medical specialists, as well as among faculty in medicine and those in other scientific fields, or between the sciences and the humanities.

Another of the factors contributing to this chasm is the lingering resentment of many faculty toward their medical school colleagues, whom they often have viewed as awash in money and able, if they were willing, to transfer vast sums of wealth to their impecunious colleagues. A few university medical centers are doing phenomenally well, and their robust balance sheets are contributing to this resentment. For example, in 2006 the CEOs of teaching hospitals at the University of Pittsburgh, Columbia University, Case Western Reserve University, and Northwestern University received annual compensation ranging from $3.3 million to $7.5 million—with an average salary of $5.0 million.[2] But these are some exceptions to the rule. The generally increasing reliance on academic health centers to care for those who are medically indigent —in addition to skyrocketing rates for medical malpractice insurance, the aggressive practice of defensive medicine laced with frequently unneeded tests to avoid lawsuits, and substantial elevation of the costs of ever more sophisticated technology, which both the lay public

and medical professionals are increasingly eager to exploit
—have combined to alter dramatically the financial situation of most academic health centers in recent years.
Although a few teaching hospitals such as those men-
tioned above are experiencing large budget surpluses, that
is definitely not the norm. Thus it is imperative that we
avoid pitting our academic health centers against the
other entities of our universities. As Steven Wartman
has observed, there is heightened sensitivity among university leaders to the fact that the "highly competitive
national and international environment . . . renders internal dissonance within an institution a drag on resources,
spirit, and intellectual creativity. Simply put, most institutions are finding it increasingly difficult and costly to
have some of their key components working at cross
purposes."[3]

Yet another impediment to bridging the gap between
these two cultures is that extremely few presidents of
comprehensive research universities have been administrators in academic health centers. Consequently most
presidents choose to make ever-so-brief and episodic for-
ays into the unfathomable abyss of IRBs, clinical trials,
complex medical practice plans, shifting reimbursement
policies, myriad insurers and billing entities, irascible
patients, prima donna subspecialists, soaring medical mal-
practice insurance premiums, and heightened security
of IT networks—especially regarding patient records. To
compound matters, there are recurring complaints about
technology and equipment that was regarded as state-
of-the-art when it was purchased but now is uniformly

derogated as hopelessly obsolescent, increasing governmental sensitivity to the adequacy of biosafety and security safeguards, histrionic protests against all animal research, and endlessly proliferating accreditation agencies, to say nothing of neighborhood opposition to expanding hospital and clinic facilities. If that weren't enough, we often witness disputes among schools within the academic center—often directed to the perceived arrogance of the medical school faculty—that generate liberal amounts of paranoia and ill will.

Once university presidents wind up in this morass, they typically perceive these dilemmas as irresolvable and say to themselves: "Help! Let me out of here. I feel more comfortable solving the myriad problems in the other parts of the university. I'll let my vice president for health affairs deal with the complex and bewildering array of problems that fester in the academic health center. I'm going to keep an arm's length from this mess." Thus they perpetuate the chasm between the two cultures.

Presidents in this circumstance typically feel an admixture of anxiety and confusion, and many cunning vice presidents for health affairs capitalize on their presidents' discomfort and naïveté by encouraging such administrative distance because it gives the academic health centers greater autonomy. This often has disastrous, albeit unintended, consequences for the entire university, in that academic health centers and their counterparts in the same institution too often wind up competing for the favor of identified philanthropists and sparring for priority in legislative appropriations. In the maelstrom of competing interests, organizational complexity, and seemingly endless bureaucratic hurdles, it is all too easy for us to lose sight of the public whose health care needs we are charged to serve.

This reflects yet another chasm, namely the persistent gap in health status and mortality between those who are affluent and those who are poor.[4] However, spanning this divide is not simply a matter of improving access to health care and making it more affordable. William Brody has astutely observed that we won't be able to remedy adequately the bedeviling problems of these two Cs—Cost and Coverage—until we "systematically address three other Cs ... Consistency, Complexity and Chronic illness."

Consistency: He notes the enormous variability in quality of care, citing a RAND survey of thirty common medical conditions in a dozen American communities, which revealed that "patients get appropriate treatment only about 55 percent of the time. In other words, only slightly more than half of the people who fall sick tomorrow will get good and appropriate care, while slightly less than half won't."

Complexity: Likening health care billing to "the modern day Tower of Babel," in which people do not speak the same language, he reports that the Johns Hopkins Hospital bills "more than 700 different players and insurers."

Chronic illness: Because "fully two-thirds of all Medicare spending is for beneficiaries who have five or more

chronic conditions," and "80 percent of all health
care costs involve patients with one or more chronic
illnesses," Brody argues: "Only when we begin to
focus systematically on disease management will
the big gains be made in better patient care and
cost reduction."

We can no longer afford to ignore these deep-seated deficiencies, which Brody accurately describes as "a patch
work quilt of different responses to different health problems."[5] Although the presidential candidates have enun-
ciated health policy positions, none has articulated a
comprehensive proposal to rectify all these profound inadequacies.

The gravity of our situation is exacerbated by the
politically popular antitax mantra, evident in the recent
federally enacted rebates as well as ubiquitous pledges
taken by politicians swearing that they will never raise
taxes. As our country gears up for the next election cycle,
pronouncements from Democrats as well as Republicans
vividly convey an even more dire prospect: those who
shout loudest the draconian chant of *cutting* taxes have
the greatest likelihood of being elected. In their call for
tax reductions to stimulate the economy, many leaders in
both parties are supporting the resurrection of supply-
side economics popularized during the Reagan administration.[6] The popular reception accorded this mantra
diminishes the already bleak prospect of a substantial
infusion of federal funds to address these health problems, and even if—mirabile dictu—additional money

were to appear, that in itself would not solve the five Cs Brody identified. Therefore we must consider a more radical approach.

Most of our academic health centers conduct scientific examination of phenomena such as disparities in health care and health status, and also train a huge proportion of our nation's health care providers. But apart from relatively isolated teams of investigators conducting large-scale intervention studies—as well as far-reaching prevention programs of one or two diseases in specified regions over extended periods—our universities generally have neither shouldered the burden to foster the policies nor initiated the comprehensive programs that will stimulate widespread and deep-seated amelioration of the prevalence of chronic illness and inadequacies in health care.

I truly believe that our universities—especially those with academic health centers—could serve as laboratories for discovering possible solutions for our nation's health care ills and create incubators in which new models of organizing and paying for health care can be tested. However, if we are to undertake this challenge, it will take a huge amount of work and require deep and genuine collaboration across institutions. That said, it is highly unlikely to happen unless a number of us who are presidents of comprehensive research universities aggressively support such a transinstitutional endeavor.

All of us research university presidents have a broad array of administrative responsibilities, and for the overwhelming majority of us that includes oversight of academic health centers. Most of us find the demands of these jobs so consuming that we feel we're doing all we can just to keep our heads above water. Together with our academic health center administrators, we are so over-whelmed by the staggering day-to-day demands of our complex organizations that we feel powerless to deal with the enormity of factors causing these health deficiencies, to say nothing of stimulating efforts to ameliorate their staggering social and economic costs. But we continue to avoid a frontal comprehensive assault on these issues at our nation's peril. We are at a critical juncture in the evolution of our ability to promote good health and provide adequate health care for our citizens.

It is high time for university presidents to collaborate with one another and our academic health center CEOs, as well as community and business leaders, to convince federal and local legislators of the enormity of these problems and persuade them to support models that will address these issues comprehensively, rather than on a piecemeal basis. Then once we have constructed such models, it is incumbent upon us to establish programs that tackle these problems. It's my sincere hope that our academic health centers will take the lead in proposing solutions to lower costs and increase coverage while simultaneously addressing frontally the three Cs Brody cites—consistency, complexity and chronic disease—and that he ominously warns are "the three riders of our health care apocalypse."[7] Unless we do so, we shall continue to be bogged down in a morass that will continue to worsen.

It is imperative that we work closely with the deans and faculty of medical schools, schools of public health, nursing schools, pharmacy schools, dental schools, and those of other health professions—in both our own and other universities—to articulate models that will not only be more equitable but will improve the health of the public and enhance access to education in the health professions. Only then will our nation's citizenry finally emerge as a truly healthy people.

NOTES

1. C. P. Snow, *The Two Cultures and the Scientific Revolution* (New York: Cambridge University Press, 1959).

2. John Carreyrov and Barbara Martinez, "Nonprofit Hospitals, Once for the Poor, Strike It Rich," *Wall Street Journal*, April 4, 2008, A1, A11.

3. Steven A. Wartman, AAHC Report from the President, August 9, 2007.

4. Robert Pear, "Gap in Life Expectancy Widens for the Nation," *New York Times*, March 23, 2008, 19.

5. William Brody, "Our Health Care Apocalypse," *Chief Executive*, March 2008, 22.

6. Louis Uchitelle, "A Political Comeback for Supply-Side Doctrine," *New York Times*, March 26, 2008, C1, C8.

7. Brody, "Our Health Care Apocalypse," 22.

TWELVE

The Role of Universities in Responding to Technological and Economic Transformation

THERE IS LIVELY DEBATE in the academy about whether or not "there must be a single overarching purpose to college." After reviewing numerous attempts to offer a unifying aim of university education, Derek Bok concludes that such attempts "take too narrow a view of the undergraduate experience." Thus he proposes several aims that "seem especially important: the ability to communicate, to think clearly and critically, to think carefully about moral issues, to fulfill their civic responsibilities, to live and work effectively with other people, to know about international affairs and about other countries and cultures, to give students a breadth of interests, and to prepare students for a career."[1]

But irrespective of whether one supports the notion of a unifying aim[2] or *à la Bok*—multiple aims[3]—the manner in which that comprehensive mission is being executed throughout the global community is undergoing unprecedented change.[4] In part that is due to the exponential rate of growth acquiring and disseminating knowledge. It is predicted that the knowledge attained during this century will exceed all that was learned in the past twenty centuries combined—and then multiplied by a factor of ten.

Concomitantly the capacity of the technologies employed to acquire and disseminate that knowledge is also growing at an exponential rate. Because of that extraordinary growth in information technology, Ray Kurzweil and Chris Meyer predict that "the 21st century will be equivalent to 20,000 years of progress at today's rate . . . which is a thousand times greater than [the rate of progress during] the 20th century." In retrospect this era will surely be regarded as the era of learners who will have spent their entire lives in a world of electronic and linked technologies that open opportunities to learn about the relation among "ecological, cultural, economic, political and technological" systems.[5]

The phenomenal expansion of knowledge and the profound impact of the technology revolution have wrought profound changes for all institutions of higher learning but especially for our research universities. As the global economy evolves in the decades ahead, the two biggest challenges our research universities will face are incorporating into the implementation of our missions and our pedagogy the extraordinary advances in the speed and extent of knowledge acquisition and dissemination; and maintaining a healthy balance between exploiting the globalization of our economies by promoting partnerships among universities—as well as between universities and industries—while not allowing these alliances to dictate the nature of our enterprise or compromise fidelity to our respective missions.

With respect to the first challenge, our students—weaned on technologically sophisticated media—are demanding better quality instruction, particularly in the delivery of our pedagogy. But the resources that we are able to devote to instruction are increasingly constrained. Especially for those of us in American public universities, the legislative bodies who support us are reducing their financial support while simultaneously demanding increased efficiency. S. Marginson argues that "better efficiency and quality . . . is the virtuous ideal glowing at the core of micro-economic reform in higher education." There is considerable hyperbole in Marginson's argument. But it is undeniable that many institutions are responding to fiscal pressure from their legislatures and boards of trustees by positing that the romantic nineteenth-century model of Mark Hopkins, perched on one end of a log with a student on the other, should be replaced by the use of highly organized instruction with large numbers of students using sophisticated technology. Admittedly any research university that aspires to be integral to the global village in the twenty-first century must plan strategically to use the myriad new technologies effectively and efficiently while realizing that, although individuals and societies may view life differently, there are "common needs and wants" that transcend political boundaries.[6]

Regrettably many research universities—faced with massive and growing enrollments—are succumbing to the notion that these sweeping changes in our pedagogy pose no threat to the integrity of our respective missions. But as Levine warns, it's easy for us to get caught up in the fervor accompanying the technological revolution without thoughtful examination of its relation to our overarching aims. He observes: "The biggest danger is that higher education may be the next railroad industry, which built bigger and better railroads decade after decade because that's the business it thought it was in. The reality was that it was in the transportation industry, and it was nearly put out of business by airplanes. Colleges and universities are not in the campus business, but the education business."[7] Although students and faculty exhibit finely tuned sensitivity to the social transformation all about us, many show that they are blissfully unaware of Levine's admonition. In the face of this diffidence we must insist that "universities are still about teaching and learning, among teachers and students, in a democratic, cross-cultural community based on mutual respect rather than hierarchy."[8]

With respect to our second challenge, perhaps the most critical issue before us as we willingly or not participate in the process of globalization is determining how to engage these dramatic changes in a manner that builds on our historic mission and does not erode our institutional integrity. The threat to the maintenance of that integrity comes principally from two sources. The first source is the students and entrepreneurs who come to our doors focused on vocational preparation, wanting us to align our institutional goals with the demands of the global marketplace. Our respective societies—particularly our students and their families—are enthusiastically embracing globalization. A corollary of this uncritical acceptance is that huge pressure is placed on our universities to develop and sustain curricula that will prepare our students for vocations in the global economy. Thus we are witnessing an unprecedented proliferation of colleges, universities, and business schools throughout the world.

Under the rubric of "increased relevance," students clamor to transform our universities into twenty-first century analogues of the medieval guilds of tradesmen in western Europe,[9] offering curricula they believe will optimize their career offerings. Although many of our graduates will indeed be employed by corporations propelling these gargantuan social and economic changes—and some of our alumni will undoubtedly spearhead these entities—the primary purpose of our universities is to afford a broad, comprehensive education for those who do not desire to be employed in shaping this transformation as well as those who do.[10]

The source of the second threat to our institutional integrity derives from the faculty and students wanting the university's research portfolio to be oriented heavily to the marketplace demands of the new millennium. But if a university wishes to expand entrepreneurial opportunities for its faculty, staff, and students while simultaneously maintaining fidelity to its mission, it will take tremendous energy and commitment by all members of the community, especially those of us in university administration. There is no question that commercial incentives and the forces of capitalism—as well as the concomitant drive to vocational preparation—have become increasingly evident on our campuses.[11] In this environment, nurtured by powerful global forces, we must be ever vigilant to any threat to erode the basic values of the academy. Over a decade ago "Kit" Lasch presciently warned against "corporate control that has diverted social resources from the humanities into military and technological research," which reveals "the university's assimilation into the corporate order."[12]

If we embark thoughtfully on initiatives made possible through the global knowledge revolution, we may sustain the integrity of our mission. But a balancing act is required to do so. On the one hand, it is essential that we address the inherent tension between sustaining the mandate to conduct scholarly investigations that lead to new knowledge in the humanities and social sciences, as well as the physical and biological sciences and engineering. Much of this scholarship will have absolutely no commercial benefit. On the other hand, we can at the same time sponsor research that offers abundant opportunity for translating intellectual property to commercial products, such as discovering drugs to attack the ravages of HIV infection and AIDS.

In order to equip our students to use our university resources most effectively as they embark on their respective careers, it is important that we take advantage of every available mechanism to overcome the traditional limitations of geography, space, and time to make our educational programs easily accessible. Mountain ranges and vast oceanic expanses were perceived by our respective ancestors as permanent and insurmountable barriers. These geographic hurdles—concomitant with the parochialism and xenophobia prevalent at that time and abetted by the extant primitive technology—kept our cultures apart for centuries. Clearly the cataclysmic advances in transportation and communication as well as substantial shifts in political ideology have reduced or eliminated the barriers that formerly separated us.

Thomas Friedman has described the phenomenon of globalization, which renders these historic barriers irrelevant: "There is something about the flattening of the world that is going to be qualitatively different from other such profound changes: the speed and breadth with which it is taking hold. This flattening process is happening at warp speed and directly or indirectly touching a lot more people on the planet at once. The great challenge for our time will be to absorb these changes in ways that do not overwhelm people but also do not leave them behind. None of this will be easy. But this is our task."[13]

If we choose, our research universities all over the world may play an absolutely pivotal role in addressing this task. The flat world requires people who not only have the ability to find and retain pertinent data, but who also can analyze the wealth of available information and efficiently develop concepts and generalizations to solve problems. Technology is evolving so rapidly that the half-life of knowledge in many domains is measured in months. But the ability to think creatively and to use information productively is measured in lifetimes.

The precursors of our present-day universities in Taiwan and the United States were established continents
apart and centuries ago by clusters of scholars and their
devotees, galvanized in the search for knowledge, wisdom,
clarity of thought, and the ability to communicate effectively. But as the pejorative term "ivory tower" connotes,
they were usually isolated from communities of scholars
in other cultures. These scholars, more often than not,
were oriented to the regions in which they labored and
disparaged sustained discourse with scholars in other
academies. Many shunned those in their respective communities who were not members of the academy.

To my mind a wonderfully eloquent yet succinct challenge to this institutional insularity was given by the his-
torian Richard Hofstadter in his commencement address
at Columbia University in 1968, delivered amid the chaos
arising from the occupation of several university buildings by student protesters and their subsequent mass
arrest: "The delicate thing about the university is that it
has a mixed character, that it is suspended between its
position in the external world, with all its corruption and
evils and cruelties, and the splendid world of our imagi-
nation."[14]

Our research universities derive much benefit from
those who transcend the world of the mind and the world
of the marketplace. Because of the influence of such persons, much of our institutional insularity has dissipated.
But as that has occurred, our universities face in more
palpable ways than ever before the temptation to allow
initiatives sponsored by knowledge-revolution-driven

industries to determine our curricula, define the criteria by which faculty are selected, and reshape our vision.

The unparalleled growth of users of the new technologies, combined with the truly remarkable speed at which our global economy is evolving, threaten to overwhelm thoughtful reflection and deliberative planning for our institutional goals. We do well to remember that although scientific discovery stimulates the development of the goods and services of information-age corporations, their products are instruments to improve the quality of life our citizens enjoy. But the development of the products is not the goal of our educational system. They are a consequence of the means by which some of our scholarship is conducted, but surely not our ends.

In the midst of the ubiquitous push toward globalization, it is essential that we preserve the sanctity of the university as "a center of intellectual life that sustains a lively, self-reflective relation to the large world."[15] We must remind ourselves daily not to allow the technoglobalization tail to wag the university dog. While our universities have clearly played a role in facilitating this global revolution, "they are more than mere places of learning."[16] We are obligated to equip our students to function as conscientious citizens, adding value to their respective communities and in doing so, enhancing the quality of our global society. "An academic degree should not be a hunting license only for self-advancement, but an indication of abilities to seek, cultivate, and sustain a richer common weal. It is not enough to achieve cultural literacy; we must engender social concern."[17]

In *Crossing the Divide*, Kofi Annan—former secretary general of the United Nations—wrote: "Today, globalization, migration, integration, communication and travel are bringing different races, cultures and ethnicities into ever closer contact with each other. More than ever before, people do understand that they are being shaped by many cultures and influences, and that combining the familiar with the foreign can be a source of powerful knowledge and insight. People can and should take pride in their particular faith or heritage. But we can cherish what we are, without hating what we are not."[18] This observation is highly compatible with the UNESCO Declaration on Higher Education, which urges our institutions to play a pivotal societal role: "Universities have a social responsibility to play an active role to make a better ... more peaceful and equitable world." Indeed, one of the principal roles of education in our respective countries is "promoting active citizenship as a condition for full participation in society."[19]

Our universities clearly can play a pivotal role in fostering the emergence of a truly global society. Taiwan and the United States have a time-honored tradition of academic exchange. It is absolutely critical that we build on this tradition as we develop long-term partnerships among our colleges and universities with government and private sector partners in our respective countries while we simultaneously work toward finding solutions to important social and economic issues facing today's highly interdependent world. If we wish to offer ideas and practices that make our institutions highly attractive to students, all our education and training programs need to be of high quality and—to the extent possible—delivered in multilingual formats with truly global accessibility.[20]

Ironically the university in medieval Europe—after which research universities in North America are modeled—was "perceived as a highly international institution," transcending national and "territorial frontiers." Indeed that institution emerged as a collection of guilds of students from nations other than those in which the university was located.[21] In moving away from the parochialism that regrettably has characterized much of higher education in recent centuries, we have much to learn from our counterparts in the corporate sector, of whom Peter Drucker observed: "In the new mental geography created by the railroad [in the Industrial Revolution], humanity mastered distance. In the mental geography of e[lectronic]-commerce, distance has been eliminated. There is only one economy and only one market. The competition is not local anymore—it knows no boundaries."[22] Businesses now enter worldwide markets overnight, and global commerce ventures allow corporations to deploy resources and management operations to any corner of the world on a moment's notice. Our universities need to emulate their nimbleness in delivering our educational offerings.

I first visited Taiwan in 1983, and I have visited your country many times since then. Our University of South Carolina faculty have several cooperative research and educational programs in place with our colleagues at

Taiwanese universities. For example, two months from now, eighteen of our students will enroll in a program at Ming Chuan entitled "Taiwan in Global Context." The sister relationship between the State of South Carolina and Taiwan enables us to offer greatly reduced tuition to Taiwanese students who enroll at our university. We also envisage research collaboration with Taiwanese scientists, international conferences, and visiting professorships. In doing so, we blend the best of both countries as our faculty and students invest their knowledge in economic and social transformation. "Information, and the knowledge that can flow from it, is more than ever the lifeblood of our economy and culture, so we must all become much more sophisticated consumers of it."[23]

In this era of the flat world, no single university and no solitary nation has a monopoly on the knowledge required to solve all the problems we face. However, by working together—collaborating from one end of the flattened earth to the other—we can accomplish far more than if we worked in splendid isolation from our sister institutions. The synergies to be gained by sharing our resources offer virtually limitless possibilities. It is imperative that we university presidents assiduously promote truly global opportunities for our institutions. In undertaking such programs, we must underscore the benefits that accrue to all participants.

We have much to learn from each other. The principal impediments to the realization of this vision of global collaboration are shrinking from boldness of purpose and succumbing to the forces of parochialism and myopia. I pray that we will have the courage to sound a clarion call for cooperation among our nations that will produce scholarly collaboration and exchanges of faculty and students—cooperation that is completely unprecedented not only in its scope but also in its magnitude. The Confucian heritage of regarding education as a cherished virtue has been consistently evident in my visits over the past quarter century to numerous Taiwanese universities, and it is abundantly evident at Ming Chuan University.

Together we will accomplish wonderful things. I sincerely believe that this conference offers concrete evidence that all of us have taken several steps in what I am confident will be a long yet highly productive journey.

NOTES

1. Derek Bok, *Our Underachieving Colleges* (Princeton: Princeton University Press, 2006), 58.

2. A variety of views on this topic are presented by Bruce Wilshire, *The Moral Collapse of the University: Professionalism, Purity, and Alienation* (Albany: State University of New York Press, 1990), xxiv. Charles W. Anderson, *Prescribing the Life of the Mind: An Essay on the Purpose of the University, the Aims of Liberal Education, the Competence of Citizens, and the Cultivation of Practical Reason* (Madison: University of Wisconsin Press, 1993), 4. Bill Readings, *The University in Ruins* (Cambridge, Mass.: Harvard University Press, 1996), 6. Stanley Fish, "Aim Low," *Chronicle of Higher Education*, May 16, 2003, C5.

3. Bok, *Our Underachieving Colleges*, 67–78.

4. Panel on the Impact of Information Technology on the Future of the Research University, *Preparing for the Revolution:*

Information Technology and the Future of the Research University (Washington, D.C.: National Academics Press, 2002), 5.

5. Ray Kurzweil and Chris Meyer, "Understanding the Accelerating Rate of Change," http://www.kurzweilai.net/meme/fram.html?main=/articles/art0563.html

6. S. Marginson, "Competition and Contestability in Australian Higher Education, 1987–1997," *Australian Universities Review* 40, no. 1 (1997): 5. L. McCabe, "Global Perspective Development," *Education* 118 (Fall 1997): 41–47.

7. Arthur Levine, "The Soul of a New University," *New York Times*, March 13, 2000, A25.

8. A. Welch, "Globalization, Post-Modernity and the State: Comparative Education Facing the Third Millennium," *Comparative Education* 37, no. 4 (2001): 487.

9. Hastings Rashdall, *The Universities of Europe in the Middle Ages*, 3 vols. (Oxford: Oxford University Press, 1936), 1: 163.

10. Paige Porter and Lesley Vidovich, "Globalization and Higher Education Policy," *Educational Theory* 50 (Fall 2000): 449–65.

11. Eyal Press and Jennifer Washburn, "The Kept University," *Atlantic Monthly* 285 (March 2000).

12. Christopher Lasch, *The Revolt of the Elites and the Betrayal of Democracy* (New York: Norton, 1995), 193.

13. Thomas L. Friedman, *The World Is Flat* (New York: Farrar, Straus & Giroux, 2005), 46.

14. David Brown, *Richard Hofstadter: An Intellectual Biography* (Chicago: University of Chicago Press, 2006).

15. L. Ilon and N. McGinn, "Education, Honesty, and Globalization," *Comparative Education Review* no. 41 (August 1997): 359.

16. H. Vessuri, "Reconciling the Local and the Global," in *The Wealth of Diversity: The Role of Universities in Promoting*

Dialogue and Development (N.p.: International Association of Universities, 2005), 113–20.

17. Edward LeRoy Long Jr., *Higher Education as a Moral Enterprise* (Washington, D.C.: Georgetown University Press, 1992), 221.

18. G. Picco et al., *Crossing the Divide—Dialogue among Civilizations* (New York: United Nations, 2001), 11.

19. Cited in Karen Holbrook, "The Role of Higher Education Institutions in Promoting Development," in *The Wealth of Diversity*, 81–91.

20. R. Craig, "Globalization and Higher Education," *Proteus* 23, no. 1 (2006): 24. U. Teichler, "The Changing Debate on Internationalization of Higher Education," *Higher Education* 48 (2004): 5–26.

21. Jurgen Enders, "Higher Education, Internationalization, and the Nation-State," Higher Education 47 (2004): 364. Rashdall, *The Universities of Europe in the Middle Ages*, 1:161.

22. P. F. Drucker, "Beyond the Information Revolution," *Atlantic Monthly* 284 (October 1999): 47–57.

23. Peter J. M. Nicholson, "The Intellectual and the Infosphere," *Chronicle Review*, March 9, 2007, B7.

Personal Coda

THIRTEEN

Reflections of Scotland on the Occasion of the Professor and Mrs. Roy Gift of the Burns Collection to the Thomas Cooper Library

UPON GRADUATING FROM COLLEGE, I decided to follow in the footsteps of my father, a Presbyterian minister. I began my theological studies at the University of Edinburgh. Because Scotland is the only country in the world in which the state church is Presbyterian, to aspiring Presbyterian clergy studying in Edinburgh is analogous to Roman Catholic seminarians heading for Rome or rabbinical scholars going to Jerusalem. Imagine my delight upon arriving in Edinburgh to be appointed student assistant to the minister of the Kirk of the Canongate. That church, located a mere five hundred yards from the Holyrood Palace, the queen's official residence in Scotland's capital, is her parish kirk when she is in Edinburgh. The minister whom I served had the title of "Chaplain to Her Brittanic Majesty in Scotland," so by extension I could stretch the point greatly and claim that I was an assistant to the queen's chaplain.

Parenthetically very few Anglicans or Episcopalians know that, when Queen Elizabeth leaves Buckingham Palace for Balmoral Castle in Scotland, her family's favorite, the instant she crosses the Scottish border she becomes the titular head of the Church of Scotland and thus a card-carrying Presbyterian. In other words she is a one-woman ecumenical movement.

The University of South Carolina has Scottish threads woven into the very warp and woof of its history, from its earliest days down to the present. Professor George Armstrong Wauchope, a Scottish American professor who joined the Carolina faculty in 1898, was given the use of one of the two side-by-side duplexes erected on the Horseshoe in 1810 and then rebuilt after a fire in 1854. Professor Wauchope was such a beloved English teacher that in 1911 the duplex he occupied came to be called Wauchope House. His long tenure there is memorialized by the white brick letters GAW embedded in the walkway in front of the abutting duplexes we now call the President's House.

Professor Wauchope wrote the lyrics of our university's alma mater and set it to the tune of "Flow Gently, Sweet Afton," whose original lyrics were composed by none other than Bobby Burns, whose birthday we celebrate today. Parenthetically Burns's letters to his true love, Clarinda—who is buried in the graveyard of the Kirk of the Canongate—are housed in the Thomas Cooper Library.

To the best of my knowledge, I am the third University of South Carolina president who was a student at the University of Edinburgh. The first, Robert Henry, who received his master of arts degree there, served as Carolina's president from 1842 to 1845. He was succeeded by William Campbell Preston—after whom Preston College, immediately behind the President's House, is named. Preston also studied at Edinburgh, and was president of Carolina from 1846 to 1851.

The heritage of the Scots at the University of South Carolina is reflected further in the fact that the largest collection of Scottish literature anywhere in the world outside Scotland is at the University of South Carolina. Scholars from six different Scottish universities—as well as from Germany, Italy, Switzerland, Canada, Australia, New Zealand, and South Africa—have come to our university to conduct research into Scottish literature. Our university has also published the world's major journal in Scottish literature, *Studies in Scottish Literature*, for more than forty years.

My introduction to Scottish lore during my memorable year as a divinity student at the University of Edinburgh—partly through a course on the history of the Church of Scotland, and in greater measure from countless conversations with my Scottish classmates, the pastor and parishioners I served, as well as numerous other friends—left an indelible impression on me. I am eternally grateful to the Scots for their warm reception of this Scandinavian American. The unfailing graciousness and consistently warm spirit of the Scots is vividly etched in my mind, and to this day those memories cause tears to well up in my eyes every time the bagpipers begin their haunting, piercing rendition of "Scotland the Brave."

Here's to Scotland; here's to the University of South Carolina; and—most especially—here's to Professor and Mrs. Roy.

NOTE

I am indebted to Patrick Scott for the meticulous research into his impressive physical and intellectual warehouse of arcana and memorabilia that enabled me to put little known bits and pieces together in a somewhat coherent manner.

This piece includes remarks given at the 277th annual meeting of the St. Andrew's Society of Charleston, South Carolina, November 30, 2006.